Praise for *Dare to Serve*

"*Dare to Serve* stands out as one of the most practical, useful books on leadership that I have ever read—full of real-world examples and grounded in the dramatic turnaround of Popeyes Louisiana Kitchen restaurants. Cheryl shares with us how to serve others with intention, competence, character, courage, and humility. Her practical experience, proven results, and contagious passion to serve others well is an inspiration to all of us who want to make a real difference in the world."

—**Bonnie Wurzbacher, former Chief Resource Development Officer, World Vision International, and former Senior Vice President, Global Customer Leadership, The Coca-Cola Company**

"*Dare to Serve* chronicles both the remarkable turnaround story of Popeyes Louisiana Kitchen, Inc., and Cheryl's inspiring personal journey of discovery, which galvanized her commitment to an unconventional approach to corporate leadership that has yielded remarkable results."

—**Andy Stanley, founder, North Point Ministries, Inc.**

"*Dare to Serve* offers a candid, behind-the-scenes look at how a struggling restaurant chain was transformed into a soaring brand success through a simple but revolutionary model of leadership based on serving others. This book is a must-read for leaders of all kinds!"

—**Phil Cordell, Global Head, New Brand Development, Hilton Worldwide**

"Compelling and inspiring! Bachelder makes the case for her people-focused approach to leadership through her real-life experience at Popeyes Louisiana Kitchen. Developed and honed in an industry where service to others is at the very core of what we do, these lessons are sure to translate not only across industries but to our personal lives as well."

—**Dawn Sweeney, President and CEO, National Restaurant Association**

"Cheryl Bachelder's brave and unconventional approach to the turnaround of Popeyes challenges all of us to step up our game. Cheryl stands in the gap for us, calling us to a purpose that will drive better results for our organizations, while putting the needs of our people and customers ahead of our own."

—**Scott MacLellan, CEO, TouchPoint Support Services, a Compass Group company**

"By focusing on the purpose-driven success of those she leads, paradoxically, Cheryl Bachelder gets the results we all want from our organizations. *Dare to Serve* is about the gutsy principles she applied to a business desperately in need of a turnaround and the spectacular results she achieved."

—Tim Irwin, PhD, bestselling author of *Impact*, *Derailed*, and *Extraordinary Influence*

"This book turned my thinking upside-down. Cheryl shares her road-tested wisdom and shows how and why Dare-to-Serve leadership works so brilliantly. This is a game-changing book and should be required reading for all leaders."

—Art Barter, President and CEO, Datron Holdings, Inc., and founder and CEO, Servant Leadership Institute

"*Dare to Serve* is a game changer! The principles outlined create exponential results far beyond what the individual ego will allow. Boards today are looking for Dare-to-Serve type leaders to ignite possibilities in their organizations. This is a must-read for leaders everywhere!"

—Jane Edison Stevenson, Vice Chairman, Board & CEO Services, Korn Ferry, and coauthor of *Breaking Away*

"Buy this book, read it, and put it to work. Cheryl is an impressively successful chief executive who has advanced the cause of servant leadership by sharing her practical, how-to approach. In doing so, she invites you to join us in building a community of serving leaders that create great workplaces and deliver superior results."

—Ken Jennings, CEO, Third River Partners, and bestselling coauthor of *The Serving Leader*

"Cheryl Bachelder has gone far beyond researching and writing about the principles of purpose-driven leadership; she has lived it in her turnaround of Popeyes. Her book *Dare to Serve* offers an authentic and compelling voice to the practice of servant leadership and serves as an inspiring example of leadership principles valuable to every company in every industry and at every stage of development."

—Idalene "Idie" Kesner, Dean, Kelley School of Business, and Frank P. Popoff Chair of Strategic Management, Indiana University

DARE
TO **SERVE**

HOW TO DRIVE SUPERIOR RESULTS
BY SERVING OTHERS

CHERYL BACHELDER

Berrett–Koehler Publishers, Inc.
a BK Business book

Berrett-Koehler Publishers, Inc.
1333 Broadway, Suite 1000
Oakland, CA 94612-1921
Tel: (510) 817-2277   Fax: (510) 817-2278   www.bkconnection.com

Ordering Information

Quantity sales. Special discounts are available on quantity purchases by corporations, associations, and others. For details, contact the "Special Sales Department" at the Berrett-Koehler address above.

Individual sales. Berrett-Koehler publications are available through most bookstores. They can also be ordered directly from Berrett-Koehler: Tel: (800) 929-2929; Fax: (802) 864-7626; www.bkconnection.com

Orders for college textbook/course adoption use. Please contact Berrett-Koehler: Tel: (800) 929-2929; Fax: (802) 864-7626.

Distributed to the U.S. trade and internationally by Penguin Random House Publisher Services.

Popeyes®, Popeyes® Louisiana Kitchen, Inc. and other associated marks are trademarks owned by Popeyes® Louisiana Kitchen, Inc. Other trademarks belong to their respective owners.

Berrett-Koehler and the BK logo are registered trademarks of Berrett-Koehler Publishers, Inc.

Printed in the United States of America

Berrett-Koehler books are printed on long-lasting acid-free paper. When it is available, we choose paper that has been manufactured by environmentally responsible processes. These may include using trees grown in sustainable forests, incorporating recycled paper, minimizing chlorine in bleaching, or recycling the energy produced at the paper mill.

Library of Congress Cataloging-in-Publication Data
Names: Bachelder, Cheryl, author.
Title: Dare to serve : how to drive superior results by serving others / Cheryl Bachelder.
Description: Second edition. | Oakland, CA : Berrett-Koehler Publishers, [2018]
    Includes bibliographical references and index.
Identifiers: LCCN 2018024636 | ISBN 9781626562356 (pbk.)
Subjects: LCSH: Leadership. | Servant leadership. | Organizational effectiveness.
Classification: LCC HD57.7 .B322 2018 | DDC 658.4/092--dc23
LC record available at https://lccn.loc.gov/2018024636

Second Edition
25 24 23 22 21 20 19 18   10 9 8 7 6 5 4 3 2 1

Book producer: Seventeenth Street Studios, copyediting: Todd Manza, text design: Nancy Koerner, cover design: Berry Design/Susan Malikowski, DesignLeaf

To my grandparents,
Jack and Bertha, John and Gertrude;
to my parents, Max and Marge;
to my siblings, Beth, Laura, and David
and their spouses;
to my husband, Chris, and daughters,
Tracy, Kathleen, and Katerina;
to sons-in-law and grandchildren,
current and future—
because of you I know the joy of love,
family, and faith.

To the Popeyes leadership team, with whom
I have served—I am deeply grateful for your
competence, your character, and your service.

To the entire Popeyes family for making
this story possible—it was amazing
to be on this journey with you.

All glory be to God the Father,
for He sent His Son, who dared to serve us all.

Contents

THE **DARE-TO-SERVE** LEADER

AT THE BEGINNING OF A BROADWAY SHOW, the lights dim, the music plays, and the audience waits for the spotlight to hit the stage. When the main actor appears, the story begins.

So it is with leadership. When you become a leader, people wait for you to step into the spotlight on center stage. All eyes are fixed on you—waiting to see who you are, what you will say, and what you will do. After all, you are the leader.

What if the spotlight appeared on stage, and you were not in it? What would happen then?

The people would be confused. They would wonder where you were. They would think that you didn't understand your role.

Until they realized what you were doing.

You are a different kind of leader. Not seeking the spotlight.

In fact, you have walked off the stage to find the light crew.

You will shift the focus of the spotlight—to the people you have been asked to lead.

1

You will lead the people to daring destinations—far beyond their imaginations.

You will focus intensely on serving them well on the journey.

You will help them discover meaning in their work and principles in their actions.

You will dare to serve.

THE SPOTLIGHT PROBLEM

Conventional leadership thinking puts the leader in the spotlight.

Conventional leaders assume the power position and declare a new vision. Grabbing the spotlight, these leaders have all the answers. They are high achievers, though perhaps a bit self-absorbed. We tolerate that, because they are going places that we want to go. If they are successful, we will be successful. So we think.

At the other extreme, we think of humble, servant leaders. They shun the spotlight. They listen carefully to the people. They involve the people in decisions. They make decisions that serve the people well. They give others credit. We wonder about these leaders. We like them, but we fear they will not get us to success. Could they deliver superior performance results? We doubt it.

We conclude that it is the leader *in the spotlight* who delivers results. Because, of course, nice guys finish last.

Have you worked for a leader who loves the spotlight? Were *you* served well?

My message is simple, but unconventional. If you move yourself out of the spotlight and dare to serve others, you will deliver superior performance results.

Most haven't heard this before. Many will be skeptical, even confused.

What about you?

Perhaps you think selfless service is for charitable causes and saints. Perhaps you think serving is weak and cowardly, not bold and courageous. Perhaps you think, *I've never met this kind of leader and doubt that they exist.*

It's time to reconsider your assumptions.

This is a different kind of leader, with a rare combination of traits, *courageous* enough to take the people to a daring destination yet *humble* enough to selflessly serve others on the journey. The dynamic tension between daring and serving creates the conditions for superior performance.

This is a Dare-to-Serve leader.

THE DISCOVERY

There's nothing fundamentally wrong with our country except that the leaders of all our major organizations are operating on the wrong assumptions.

ROBERT TOWNSEND, *UP THE ORGANIZATION*

About fifteen years ago, I began to study leadership with a newfound intensity. At the time, I had been working for large public companies for twenty years. I had been promoted numerous times and had worked for a wide range of people—some great leaders and some terrible leaders.

I started looking at the traits of the leaders I had loved—the ones for whom I had worked the hardest, the ones who had brought out my best performance. I discovered that the leaders I admired most not only were great to work for but also led their teams to remarkable results.

What kind of leader would I aspire to become? What model would I follow?

In my leadership journey, I have uncovered something that, in your heart of hearts, you already know.

Your favorite leaders have been decidedly different. Their motives go beyond self-interest. They challenge you to pursue daring, bold aspirations that create an exciting place to work. They shun the spotlight in favor of serving a higher purpose. They evidence principles in their daily decisions. You not only love these leaders but also perform your very best for them.

So now the question is, what kind of leader will you choose to be? Will you dare to serve?

THIS BOOK IS FOR YOU

This book is for practitioners—people leading right now—in any organization, large or small, at any level. If you have been given a position to lead people, this book is for you.

The inspiration for this book is not a group of famous leaders, chief executive officers, or celebrities but ordinary people who want to do extraordinary things wherever they are given the opportunity to lead—at work, at home, or in the community. I was privileged to meet these inspirational people daily during my work with the people who led Popeyes restaurants, from New Orleans, Louisiana, to Singapore. Restaurant leaders dare to serve far more often than do the CEOs I have met. They have inspired me to tell this story.

WHAT WILL YOU LEARN?

This book brings together the discoveries of my leadership journey in the hope that this perspective can help you become a Dare-to-Serve leader with superior performance results. What I propose is not an impossible dream, but it is unconventional thinking.

The first half of the book is the story of the turnaround of Popeyes Louisiana Kitchen, Inc., a publicly traded global restaurant chain I am honored to have led. The Popeyes story provides a real-world example of how one leadership team dared to serve the people well—and produced industry-leading results.

The second half of the book is about how you can become a Dare-to-Serve leader. It offers thoughts and reflections to guide you in becoming the most effective leader you can be.

What is the most difficult thing I will suggest to you?

You will have to take yourself out of the spotlight.

The curtain will open, the lights will dim, and the people will be waiting.

You will not do the expected. You will not step into the spotlight.

Instead, you will find a way to get that spotlight to shine on others. You will help them pursue dreams and find meaning in work. You will grow their capabilities. You will model principles in daily decisions that build an environment of trust and commitment. When the people figure out what you are doing, they will find that you are a leader they want to follow on a path to the best performance results of their life.

If you become a Dare-to-Serve leader, your legacy will be your impact on the lives of the people you lead and the outstanding results you create together.

WHERE DID I GET THIS IDEA?

Many years ago, I met Jim Collins, the author of *Good to Great*, at a meeting of Yum! Brands leaders. He presented the findings of his book, describing a new type of top-performing leader: a Level 5 leader. He said that Level 5 leaders are a "paradoxical mix of personal humility and professional will. They are ambitious, to be sure, but ambitious first and foremost for the company, not themselves."

Collins's work established a case for servant leadership called by another name, the Level 5 leader. It included financial data proving that Level 5 leaders delivered superior performance results.

The idea fascinated me.

I wondered, *Is it possible to be humble and ambitious? What would it mean to put the people and the enterprise first—above self-interest? How would this inspire superior performance?*

Collins's book sold more than 2.5 million copies. But will these findings change your approach to leadership?

THE OPPORTUNITY ARRIVES

In 2007, I got my chance to test Dare-to-Serve leadership in a real-world setting with seven talented people, collectively called the Popeyes leadership team.

We made a daring decision to serve others well by pursuing a bold ambition for the enterprise. We then established a purpose and a set of principles to govern our leadership.

We wanted to prove that we could drive superior performance results by leading like the handful of humble, serving leaders we read about in books like *Leadership Is an Art*, *The Soul of the Firm*, and *Firms of Endearment*. At the time, Popeyes was a struggling restaurant chain with a long history of declining sales and profits. It offered a classic "turnaround" opportunity. Leadership had been a revolving door of short-lived CEOs—four in seven years.

In those same seven years, guest traffic had declined. Same-store sales were negative. Restaurant average unit volume and profitability had fallen to dangerously low levels. New restaurant returns were anemic. The relationship between the company and its franchisees was on the rocks. As for investors, the stock price had slid from a peak of $34 per share, in 2002, to $13 on the day I joined the company.

What better time for a grand experiment in leadership? What if we were able to prove that a daring aspiration and selfless service to others could deliver superior performance results? What if a purpose and a set of principles could guide us to industry-leading performance? What if we did this under the scrutiny of a public-company environment, garnering the attention of those cynical, short-term Wall Street investors?

Fast-forward to end of the story. Popeyes restaurants experienced eight years of growth. Average restaurant sales climbed by 45 percent. Market share grew from 14 to 24 percent. The profitability of Popeyes restaurants doubled in terms of real dollars, with restaurant profit margins up from 18 to 23 percent.

The franchisees were so delighted with the business results that they rapidly remodeled existing restaurants and began feverishly building new Popeyes, with excellent returns on their investment.

The corporation saw diluted earnings per share grow from $0.76 to $1.98 per share from 2008 to 2016. The stock price grew from $13 to $61 at the end of 2016, up nearly 500 percent in nine years.

During this time, the company was the darling of the industry . . . a favorite of the franchisees . . . a favorite of lenders . . . a favorite of investors . . . and a case study in serving up superior performance results.

The secret to Popeyes' turnaround performance?

We dared to serve.

HOW TO GET THE MOST FROM THIS BOOK

As I grew up, I learned many of my leadership lessons from my father. Daddy Max, as I called him. He served as vice president of National Semiconductor Corporation for many years, primarily overseeing manufacturing operations in Asia.

My dad was an accomplished and perceptive story-teller, and most of his stories were about how to lead people. Over dinner he would talk about his day at work. Always included in his story was the "moral of the story," to make sure we understood the underlying leadership lesson.

One evening my dad was pacing the kitchen floor, visibly upset. When I asked him what was bothering him, he told me that tomorrow he would be laying off people at the manufacturing plant. He told me he was sick over it. People he cared about would be unemployed. Families would suffer from the loss. Moral of the story: letting people go should make your stomach turn; never take it lightly.

My dad and mom raised four children, each of whom became a CEO or president of a company, in four different industries. The leadership lessons in those dinner table stories served us well.

Similarly, I will share leadership stories—what I have observed, reflected on, and learned. I encourage you to seek the "moral of the story," to discover the leadership lesson. Throughout these chapters, you will find Dare-to-Serve Reflections to help you think about the leadership role you are in today and the best way to influence and steward the people entrusted to your care. In this process, you will consider whether you want to be a Dare-to-Serve leader.

The world is waiting for leaders to come forward who can steward an organization's people and resources to superior performance. When you choose to humbly serve others and courageously lead them to daring destinations, the team will give you their very best performance. And the spotlight will be found shining on the remarkable results of the organization as a whole.

May you be inspired to be a Dare-to-Serve leader who drives superior results. And may you spend the rest of your days teaching others to do the same.

Cheryl A. Bachelder
Former Chief Executive Officer
Popeyes Louisiana Kitchen, Inc.

PART ONE

HOW TO DRIVE
SUPERIOR RESULTS

I have not always enjoyed success as a leader.

In the fall of 2003, unable to sustain a turnaround of KFC restaurants, my boss suggested that it was time for me to leave. In other words, I got fired.

Few things are as clarifying as losing your job. My confidence was shaken. This was supposed to be the pinnacle position of my career—my day in the spotlight.

Perhaps that was the problem. The spotlight was not where I was supposed to be.

After meandering through a few consulting projects, I decided that my "retirement" work would be serving on boards. I was honored to join the boards of the True Value Company and AFC Enterprises, Inc., the parent company of Popeyes.

In the spring of 2007, the CEO of Popeyes left the company. After a search committee reviewed several candidates to be the next CEO, the board asked me to lead the organization.

Looking back, this move was providential. In my previous role at KFC, I had been humbled. Now I would be given a chance to redeem that experience by leading the people of Popeyes.

I had a chance to step out of the spotlight, to lead the people to a daring destination, to serve them well along the journey, and to create the conditions for superior performance.

Popeyes' performance results were remarkable.
I only wish I had been humbled sooner.

ONE

WHOM WILL WE SERVE?

*It begins with the natural feeling
that one wants to serve, to serve first.*

ROBERT K. GREENLEAF,
THE SERVANT AS LEADER

I AM AN ETERNAL OPTIMIST, a certified member of the positive-thinking club.

When we were growing up, my mother woke my siblings and me by playing loud music on the stereo and saying, "Good morning! It's a beautiful day. Rise and shine." There was no opportunity for negativity. It was *going* to be a good day.

I continued this tradition with my children. The mantra of their childhood was "Your attitude is your altitude." They still grimace when I say it, but the message is etched in their minds. Decide how you will approach this day—and that will determine your day.

The same is true in leadership: *your attitude is your altitude.*

When I joined Popeyes, the place needed an attitude adjustment. The problem? The people we were responsible for leading were viewed as "a pain in the neck."

The franchise owners were "difficult." The restaurant teams were "poor performers." The guests were "impossible to please." The board members were "challenging." The investors were "not on our side."

The first step in turning around your organization's performance? Think positively about the people you lead. Your attitude will determine the altitude of your performance results.

DARE-TO-SERVE REFLECTION #1 *How do you think about the people you lead? Are they a "pain in the neck" or essential to the future success of the organization?*

THE BUSINESS SITUATION

Popeyes' performance in 2007 couldn't have been much worse. Every data point that we measured was going the wrong way. Sales were declining. Guest satisfaction was worst-in-class. Restaurant profits were down in absolute dollars and in margin. Morale at the company was negative. Franchise owners were mad and "sick and tired" of bad results. Investors were disappointed in the stock performance and wanted answers. The board was tired of hearing promises that did not materialize.

In the following year, economic conditions would deteriorate as well. Lehman Brothers would disappear. The stock market would fall precipitously. The United States would head into a steep recession that contributed to the slowdown of the global economy. Times were not good.

The odds were stacked against a successful Popeyes turnaround.

What leadership approach would lead to success?

NOT LIKE THEM

Picture eight members of the Popeyes leadership team stuffed in a small conference room at an Atlanta facility called the Buckhead Club. Our job for the day? To make a conscious decision on how we would lead Popeyes to sustained success.

We started by making lists of the traits we admired in the best leaders of our careers. Interestingly, the conversation quickly turned to the traits that we wanted to avoid, traits that characterized the worst leaders we had met.

On the flip chart, we listed words like *self-absorbed*, *arrogant*, and *condescending*.

Before we knew it, we were telling one another stories about the difficult people we had worked for. It became a "can you top this?" contest.

That was a turning point in our leadership of Popeyes. Our first decision: we did not want to lead like "them."

We started talking about our favorite leadership philosophies. One person mentioned a book that had been influential in his life, *Leadership Is an Art*, by Max De Pree. Published in 1989 by the then-CEO of Herman Miller, the book put forth a novel idea—that leaders are *stewards* of the people and the organizations they lead. When leaders create environments where followers thrive, the business performs well.

Others brought up books that they liked—authored by Patrick Lencioni, Stephen Covey, Jim Collins, and more—and a theme emerged in the conversation. We wanted to be leaders who *served well* the people, brand, and organization we had been given. We didn't want to fall prey to the self-focused leadership style we had observed in others. Our belief was that serving people well would generate better business results.

One member of the team said, "I think there is a name for this kind of leadership. Give me a minute to do a Web search." He was the only one with an iPhone at the time, and he quickly came up with the answer. A man named Robert Greenleaf had written about a leadership approach called "servant leadership." It was about serving the people well—above self-interest.

That's it!

Serving others over self.

We quickly agreed that this servant leadership notion would guide us going forward.

DARE-TO-SERVE REFLECTION #2 *Think about difficult leaders you have worked for. Have you made a conscious decision to lead differently than "them"?*

But there was one more thing. We believed that servant leadership would deliver superior results. The performance of the enterprise would be the evidence that we had served others well.

Before leaving the conference room that day, we had a draft of the Popeyes purpose and principles that would guide our leadership for years to come.

Our purpose: to inspire servant leaders to achieve superior results.

Our principles: six behaviors we saw as essential to serving the people well *and* delivering superior performance—passion, listening, planning, coaching, accountability, and humility.

We made a decision that day: we decided to serve.

Dare-to-Serve leaders begin by intentionally deciding on their attitude and leadership approach.

- Decide to think positively about the people you lead.

- Decide to be a leader who serves others over self-interest.

It is both courageous and humbling to remove yourself from the spotlight and shift your focus and energy toward serving others well. This is how you create an environment for superior results.

THE MANY CHOICES

If we were going to serve people well at Popeyes, *whom* would we serve?

We listed all the possibilities on the conference room flip chart: the guests, the shareholders, the franchise owners, the team members, the board of directors, the regulators, the accountants. Had we missed anyone?

Someone said, "Don't we have to serve *all* of those people?"

Hmm. Could be true. Let's go through each possibility.

In restaurants, the ultimate goal is to serve your restaurant guest well. After all, guests buy the food; without them, there is no business. If they are not served well, they don't come back.

Popeyes was a public company. Shareholders had invested in the business and expected a reasonable, preferably good, return on that investment. We were hired as their "stewards." Without their investment, we were not funded for growth. If shareholders are not well served, they exit the stock—and the stock price falls—reducing access to capital and the value of the enterprise.

Popeyes licenses to franchise owners the rights to use the brand and the operating system. These owners borrow money and invest it in building Popeyes restaurants, hiring and training restaurant crews, and building relationships with the communities and guests we serve. Without franchisees, we do not have a global restaurant chain; they drive expansion. If they are not well served, they exit the brand—selling or closing restaurants—and reduce our ability to serve guests Popeyes' famous Louisiana recipes.

DARE-TO-SERVE REFLECTION #3 *Who are the most*
important people you serve—the owner,
the boss, the customer, the employees?
Which one is your primary focus?

It takes about 60,000 team members to run the more than 2,600 restaurants around the globe. These team members get up every day, come to work, prepare the food, serve the guests, clean up the place, and close the doors. These team members feed and serve the guests. If the leadership does not serve the team members well, those team members go to work somewhere else. Without them, Popeyes is not open for business.

In business, we have many choices of people to serve; they are all important. Would we serve them equally or would we pick one as our primary focus?

THE CHOICE WE MADE

At Popeyes, we chose to serve the franchise owners well as our first priority.

In the franchising model, we make money in two basic ways: we collect royalties on restaurant sales and we collect franchise fees when a new restaurant is built. Those monies fund the infrastructure of the company so we can carry out the service obligations of the franchise contract: brand marketing, new product innovation, operating systems, quality assurance, and more.

We have long-term contracts with our franchise owners—typically twenty-year agreements with options to renew. Thus, we have long-term relationships with the owners who borrowed the money to build the restaurants and who hire the people who serve the guests. Franchise owners do the heavy lifting.

As we looked at our options for whom we would serve, we thought the franchise owners merited our immediate attention. They had made sizable investments and were committed by contract to operate our brand. If they did not prosper, there was no chance Popeyes sales would go up (generating royalties) or franchise fees would increase (from new openings). Either franchise owners would succeed or Popeyes would fail.

This decision was not typical in our industry. Franchisors and franchisees are constantly in conflict— arguing about the contract, the business strategy, the restaurant design, the promotion pricing, or the cost of the food. If the conflict gets particularly bad, threats of lawsuits quickly surface.

Soon after I joined Domino's Pizza, in 1995, Domino's franchisees sued the company in a class-action lawsuit. When I joined KFC, in February 2001, I learned of the long history of conflict between KFC franchisees and the franchisor, with a negotiated settlement in 1996. During my restaurant career, the media has reported on troubled franchisee/franchisor relationships at well-known brands such as Burger King and Quiznos, among others.

Interestingly, unresolved conflict with franchise owners never leads to operational excellence or superior sales and profit performance. Instead, franchise systems with high internal conflict have negative business results. It is predictable. Nonetheless, franchisees and franchisors typically don't get along.

So we asked ourselves a few questions.

What if we dared to be different from our peers? What if we dared to serve the franchise owners well?

What would that look like?

We would have to work closely with the franchisees to choose the vital few initiatives that would improve performance. Once we were aligned on the right plan, the franchise owners would implement that plan in the restaurants. When the plan was executed well by the restaurants, performance results would improve. When sales and profits improved, franchisees would build more restaurants. New restaurant growth would create value for the shareholders.

This could work.

Our success would begin and end with the success of the Popeyes franchise owners.

LOVING THOSE YOU LEAD

Here's a tough question. Do you love the people you've decided to serve?

It helps.

One Popeyes leader said it this way: "If you are in the franchising business, you should love the franchisees."

To love franchisees, you have to love entrepreneurs. Entrepreneurs are passionate. They take risks. They invest for the future. They are ambitious. They are definitely not corporate bureaucrats. They do not have much patience with people holding MBA degrees or offering up expensive, harebrained ideas. What if the most important people in your business are entrepreneurs? You must decide to love them.

As a side note, I can't imagine why someone *wouldn't* love franchise owners. I'm biased by my worldview. I believe that democratic capitalism creates conditions for entrepreneurs to invest and grow small businesses. The entrepreneurs are pursuing a dream, and owning a small business is their path to that dream. In the United States, we call this the "American Dream." People come to this country just for the chance to build their own business.

These are the people we were honored to serve at Popeyes. The Popeyes franchise owners decided to take the risk and invest sweat equity and financial capital in building and operating Popeyes restaurants. They are amazing people with equally amazing life stories.

Here are just a few examples of the many franchise owners in the Popeyes system whom I loved.

Lal Sultanzada is a Popeyes franchisee in New York City. Lal moved to this country from Afghanistan. His first job was working in a chicken restaurant in Harlem.

Eventually he saved enough money to buy that restaurant and became a Popeyes franchise owner. Today, Lal has dozens of restaurants operating to the highest of standards. His restaurant leaders win many Popeyes awards. I love that Lal has sent his children to college so that they can follow in his footsteps and run this highly successful family restaurant business.

Mack Wilbourn operates three Popeyes restaurants at the Hartsfield-Jackson Atlanta International Airport. Two of them have the largest sales volume in the system. Mack hires people who take fabulous care of the guests. You will often hear the restaurant manager, Edith, say, "Honey, you are looking good today! What can I get you for dinner?" I love the warmth and positive energy that Mack's teams bring to guests. They set the standard for service excellence.

John Broderson is a Popeyes franchisee who owns urban restaurants in Milwaukee, Chicago, Detroit, and Puerto Rico. His career began in a troubled Popeyes restaurant in Chicago that his father had purchased. Over time, John developed a talented team of restaurant leaders who routinely won awards in the system. Several years ago, John went back to Chicago to seek out that first Popeyes restaurant he worked in—and he bought it. I love the fact that John invests in urban neighborhoods, providing career opportunities to many.

Harry Stafford invested in the restaurant business after a successful career in law and Texas oil. His organization owns and operates more than a dozen Popeyes restaurants with excellence. Now in his seventies, Harry remains one of the most forward-looking entrepreneurs, buying property and expanding his Popeyes network in the Houston area. I love that Harry leads with integrity and has invested his time serving as a leader in the Popeyes system.

Amin Dhanani is the sixth son of a family that immigrated to the United States to be entrepreneurs. His family is one of the largest operators of Burger King restaurants, as well as Popeyes. This owner is one of the boldest and fastest-expanding operators in the system, owning and operating Popeyes in multiple states. I love Amin's daring aspiration for expanding Popeyes across the nation as fast as possible.

Guillermo Perales owns Popeyes restaurants in Texas and Florida. Beyond Popeyes, he is the largest Hispanic franchisee in America, owning multiple retail businesses. When Guillermo saw the turnaround of Popeyes performance results, he decided to become one of the fastest-growing developers. I love that he is willing to invest in Popeyes' future.

Danny Gililland operates Popeyes in Little Rock, Arkansas. Danny loves restaurant operating systems, and his wife, Lynda, loves training restaurant teams. The Gilillands volunteer to test just about every piece of restaurant equipment or new training process that the team comes up with. I love that Danny and Lynda never tire of debugging these inventions, and their enthusiastic efforts help us make better decisions for the system.

Nareg Amirian is a second-generation Popeyes franchisee, following his successful father, Bobken Amirian, an Armenian who emigrated from Iran. Nareg combines his experience in the family business with an MBA from the UCLA Anderson School of Management and runs restaurants in Las Vegas and Los Angeles. I love that Nareg has courageously stepped forward to run the family business for the next generation.

Now I have to pause and apologize to every Popeyes franchisee whom I did not mention. Please know that I love you, too!

DARE-TO-SERVE REFLECTION #4 *What are the specific qualities you love in the people you lead?*

We had more than three hundred franchise owners at Popeyes—and I loved them all. These were hardworking people who took bold risks to grow Popeyes and to serve our guests well. They are inspiring people, people to be admired. They deserve to be loved. They deserve to be served.

THE DIFFICULTY OF SERVING

If you choose to be a Dare-to-Serve leader, you'll have one very big obstacle to overcome.

Yourself.

It is easy to say that you want to serve others well, but it is much harder to do so in daily life.

This topic is seldom discussed out in the open. It would not be seen as admirable to admit that your leadership approach is aimed at serving *yourself* well. In fact, I've never heard anyone actually say this out loud.

Interestingly, I have heard many *followers* tell me that their leader was self-absorbed. It turns out that the people know your motive, whether *you* know it or not.

They know if you are making a decision to make yourself look good. They know if you are angling to get promoted. They know if you are hoping for a raise to buy a new house. They know your motives by your actions, not your words.

No one is unscathed by this truth. I am as guilty as anyone else. And you?

WHAT'S IN IT FOR YOU?

Even leaders who say they want to be Dare-to-Serve leaders have this question in their own head: What's in it for me? How will I benefit?

You're not a bad person for considering this question. You're just like everybody else; you think of yourself first. So let's tackle this question before going further.

Here are the five benefits to you of becoming a Dare-to-Serve leader.

Benefit to You No. 1 *People will tell you the stuff you need to know.* Self-centered leaders don't invest time in getting to know their people. When the people don't know you well, they won't tell you what is going on in the organization. You miss out on mission-critical facts that you need to make decisions. Serving the people well requires that you spend time knowing the people well.

Benefit to You No. 2 *People will be more likely to follow your bold vision.* As the leader, you are expected to create the vision for the organization. No one will debate that. But you don't actually implement the vision; you need followers who believe in your vision and are motivated to do the work. To be highly motivated, the people need to know that you have their best interests at heart. Serving the people well requires that you take their interests into account as you lead the organization.

Benefit to You No. 3 *People will actually do the stuff you need to get done without a lot of reminding.* Self-centered leaders who insist on making all the decisions make the people "leader dependent." Unable to perform on their own, the followers wait for the leader to tell them what to do. They do the minimum, unless you follow up repeatedly. Serving the people well requires that you empower the team, let them make decisions, and let them lead.

Benefit to You No. 4 *People will perform better.* Self-centered leaders create anxious, unsafe work environments where people see no apparent benefit in taking risks or growing in capability. The environment is governed by threats and fear; a scarcity mentality prevails. When work is all about the leader's own ambitions, there is no good reason to give one's best performance. In contrast, if you serve the people well, you will provide a safe environment focused on personal growth, promotion opportunities, and the fun of "winning" together. This leads to winning results.

Benefit to You No. 5 *People will watch out for you and protect you from yourself.* Self-centered leaders create the conditions for a lapse in personal integrity. The leader who receives little feedback from the team becomes overconfident, without checks and balances. The leader's compass becomes "do the right thing, as long as it advances my career." This blind spot causes the leader to miss the truly moral decisions that are right for the people and the enterprise, regardless of cost to self. The leader who serves the people well finds that the people protect you from yourself; they have your back.

WHAT MIND-SET TRAPS LIE AHEAD?

If you and your team commit to becoming Dare-to-Serve leaders, certain mind-sets will trip you up on a regular basis. Here are just a few of the mind-set traps our team experienced at Popeyes.

Mind-Set Trap No. 1: "But I am right." It is difficult to stay in a mind-set of serving others when they do not agree with you. Your first inclination is to think, *But I am right, and they are wrong.*

In leadership, and certainly in the franchising business, this happens often—we disagree with one another—but we must work together to move the business forward. We found that acting in unison as a restaurant chain always worked better than acting in disunity. Nonetheless, it was frustrating when we failed to gain alignment with the franchise owners, particularly when the facts were on our side. Our impatient "self" wished we could make the decision "solo." While that might be efficient, it would not serve franchise owners well.

In the nine years we led Popeyes, this situation occurred multiple times. We recommended a business plan that probably was sound and probably would have worked just fine. The franchise owners did not agree. We slowed down, swallowed our pride, and prioritized the *relationship* with the franchise owners over being right. We may have lost some momentum in the short term, but we gained alignment that led to a well-executed plan in the marketplace. Sometimes you must go slow to go fast.

Mind-Set Trap No. 2: "What's wrong with these followers?" One of the big challenges of leadership is getting the followers to go with you on the journey. This can be exhausting—a constant need to persuade and re-persuade the followers. It makes you wonder *Why don't they see the bold vision? Why don't they see the opportunities ahead?*

Persuading more than three hundred Popeyes franchise owners to agree on a decision was exhausting work, and when it isn't going well, your self-talk begins to say, *What is wrong with these people?* The franchising contract gave the company the right to make certain decisions; we could simply say, "It's in the contract."

That is tempting, but it is not serving. We reminded ourselves that influencing and persuading others is ultimately more effective than exercising authority over them. At Popeyes, we had a contract if we needed it, but we wanted to use it only as a last resort.

One tactic we used effectively to manage ourselves in this circumstance was this: when one of the senior leaders got "exhausted" with the process of bringing the franchisees into agreement with us, we let someone else take over who was fresh and more objective about the matter. This gave the one leader a rest and a chance to recover positive energy, while the pinch hitter led the decision to closure.

Our franchisees came to appreciate this behavior of the team. It gave them confidence that someone would always stay in the room with them to hear their input, even when one of us got tired of the topic. In fact, after many years of practice, our franchisees often requested that another leader get involved in a matter if there was difficulty getting to alignment.

Mind-Set Trap No. 3: "We wish they trusted us." Everyone knows that trust is essential to high-performing teams, but it isn't easy to attain. Once you get to trust, it can disappear in a moment's time. Why is this trust thing so difficult?

Stephen Covey taught that human beings have emotional bank accounts. If you make positive deposits over time, trust builds in the relationship. If you make negative withdrawals over time, trust erodes.

At the outset, we believed this to be true in the franchising business. Our leadership team invested in making lots of positive deposits in the trust bank account of our owners. We envisioned that each shared "win" would be a deposit that would build a high-trust partnership. Arguably, the performance results of the company alone should have built immense trust with the franchise owners.

Yet we discovered that trust does not accumulate between a franchisor and a franchisee. Trust is built for one decision, but it seldom carries forward to the next one.

At first we were discouraged by learning this—it seemed unfair and unreasonable. Our franchisees constantly reminded us of past decisions that had broken trust—there are many in a forty-three-year company history. Those memories are elephant-sized and they don't go away.

Bemoaning this lack of deserved trust is a self-serving mind-set. Instead, we encouraged one another to "be the adult." Another way to say this: we modeled what trust looks like and behaved accordingly. The Popeyes leadership team had strong emotional bank accounts with one another, and that provided the high-trust work environment we needed to be effective leaders.

I've come to understand the similarity between working with franchise owners and parenting an adopted child. Because of a history of distrust in their early life, they may never trust you, but you can still lead them, love them, and serve them well.

WHOM WILL WE SERVE?—THE PERFORMANCE RESULTS

To measure how well we kept our promise to serve the franchise owners, we conducted a survey every summer to get feedback from them. This was our report card on how we served our most important customer. Each year, the survey provided us with insight into areas of opportunity for future improvements. This feedback loop was essential to maintaining our commitment to serving the franchisees well.

Table 1 shows how we transformed the relationship with the franchise owners in the first five years of the turnaround. The overall rating of the quality of the Popeyes system remained at 94 or 95 percent satisfaction through 2016.

TABLE 1: Popeyes Franchise Owner Survey Results

Percent of franchisees rating Popeyes good, very good, or excellent

	2008	2013	Change
How would you rate the overall quality of the Popeyes system?	66	95	+29
Would you invest in Popeyes again?	76	93	+17
Would you recommend Popeyes to another potential franchisee?	67	90	+23
Popeyes is committed to a positive, long-term relationship with me.	66	91	+25
Popeyes understands that if I am successful, they are successful.	76	91	+15

DARE-TO-SERVE REFLECTION #5 *How do you gain meaningful feedback from those you serve?*

THE DECISION TO SERVE

The first decision of a Dare-to-Serve leader? You decide to serve the people well.

This decision has many benefits. Perhaps the most important is this: People who are well served are more likely to give their best to the organization. That gives you the best prospect of getting superior performance results.

Consciously decide whom you will serve.

Don't leave this to chance.

At the outset, I suggest that you focus on serving one specific group of people. You will be more intentional in your decisions to serve them well. You will be more likely to notice the challenges of serving and to make adjustments in your approach. You will be more likely to experience the benefits of superior performance.

At Popeyes, we discovered the performance power of serving others by focusing first on our franchise owners. This success gave us conviction about the importance of serving every constituent in the company well—the restaurant manager, the employee, the guest, the vendor partner, the investor, the board.

Dare-to-Serve leadership is a *mind-set* for approaching every constituent.

Bring your team together today—and decide to serve.

TWO

WHAT IS THE **DARING** DESTINATION?

The bravest are the tenderest,—the loving are the daring.
BAYARD JOSEPH TAYLOR (1825–1878)

AROUND THE DINNER TABLE, our family likes to discuss words. This habit comes from my husband of more than thirty years. He cares deeply about the proper use of words. Recently, in one of these evening discussions, we contemplated the meaning of the terms *paradox* and *oxymoron*.

A paradox is something that is made up of two opposite things and that seems impossible but is actually true or possible. The word originates from the Greek word *paradoxos*, meaning "contrary to expectation."

An oxymoron is considered a "compressed paradox." In terms I can understand, that means two words used together that are seemingly contradictory, such as "silent alarm." The origin of *oxymoron* is also Greek—a combination of two Greek words, *oxys*, meaning "sharp" or "keen," and *moros*, meaning "foolish." Sharp and foolish? It turns out that even the word *oxymoron* is an oxymoron.

So to make this dinner game more interesting, we shared our favorite oxymorons:

Live recording

Mandatory option

Jumbo shrimp

Paid volunteer

Minor crisis

To keep my head in the game, I start thinking about business:

Assistant supervisor

Friendly takeover

Limited guarantee

Working vacation

Then my mind wanders to leadership:

Daring serving

Seemingly contradictory—an oxymoron?

NO DARING DESTINATION

At the beginning of the Popeyes turnaround, there was no clearly stated destination for the people and the enterprise. The people were committed and hardworking, but they did not know where they were going. When you asked people where the organization would be in five years, they responded with either "I don't know" or "I wish I knew."

Popeyes wasn't winning any games. The team was discouraged, even exasperated. They were struggling, with no evidence of a turnaround in sight. They needed to know what tournament they were playing in. How else would they know how to prepare for a game? How would they recognize a win?

Popeyes needed a daring destination—for the people and the enterprise. What bold goals would mobilize the Popeyes team to high performance? How would we bring a daring aspiration to life for the organization?

A Dare-to-Serve leader pursues a daring destination for the people and the enterprise. You can't serve the people well if you don't have aspirations for the team to be wildly successful. The steps:

- State the daring destination with a plausible business case.

- Focus on the vital few actions, the hard things that must be addressed.

- Commit the resources needed to reach the destination, as evidence of your conviction.

- Create a work environment that brings out the best in people and performance.

- Have the courage to measure and report progress.

PROVIDING A DARING DESTINATION

"Would you tell me, please, which way I ought to go from here?"

"That depends a good deal on where you want to get to," said the Cat.

"I don't much care where," said Alice.

"Then it doesn't matter which way you go," said the Cat.

LEWIS CARROLL,
ALICE'S ADVENTURES IN WONDERLAND

The first time I met the Popeyes franchisees was at the Popeyes International Franchise Conference in Orlando, Florida—a gathering of the franchise owners and their management teams with the Popeyes leaders who support them. My first day on the job involved standing on a huge stage in front of the business owners, with a teleprompter and a PowerPoint presentation.

Looking back, I probably should have worn a bulletproof vest. With my optimistic personality, I told the franchise owners how thrilled I was to join Popeyes. I shared a few of the reasons why I thought we had a great opportunity in front of us. The most important thing I established that day was a picture of the future—a daring destination we could aspire to reach together.

The vision I shared was this:

One day Popeyes will again be the hottest concept among U.S. quick-service restaurants. We will have average unit volumes of $1.2 million. We will have quick drive-thrus that delight our guests. The franchise owners will be making 22 percent restaurant operating profit. And we will build more restaurants with good financial returns to the franchise owners. Over time, we will more than double the size of this chain.

Our aspirations for Popeyes were conveyed in a four-part plan as shown in Figure 1—we called it the Roadmap to Results. The four pillars of the plan were *build a distinctive brand, run great restaurants, grow restaurant profits,* and *accelerate quality openings.* The road map wasn't rocket science—or wildly different from our competitors' plans—but the words clearly explained what we were going to do to become a growing, prosperous restaurant chain.

We defined the future state of Popeyes. Nobody had any reason to believe we were actually going to reach those goals. Nonetheless, the franchise owners were temporarily calmed by the idea that we *had* bold goals and a vision of future success.

DARE-TO-SERVE REFLECTION #6 *What daring destination have you established for your team and organization? What strategies will ensure the team reaches the destination?*

A friend of mine says that leading a team is like taking your family on vacation. Until the family knows where they are going, they won't know whether to bring their winter coats or their bathing suits.

Define the destination so that the team can pack their suitcases.

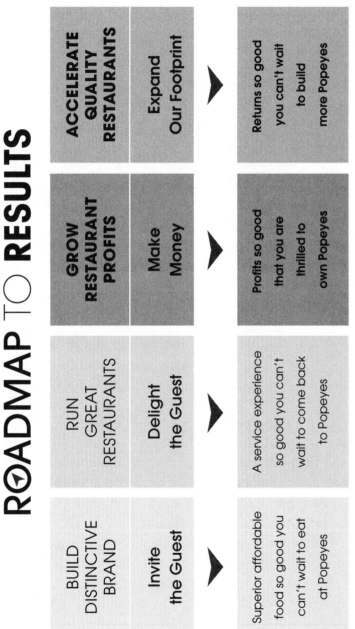

ROADMAP TO RESULTS

BUILD DISTINCTIVE BRAND	RUN GREAT RESTAURANTS	GROW RESTAURANT PROFITS	ACCELERATE QUALITY RESTAURANTS
Invite the Guest	Delight the Guest	Make Money	Expand Our Footprint
Superior affordable food so good you can't wait to eat at Popeyes	A service experience so good you can't wait to come back to Popeyes	Profits so good that you are thrilled to own Popeyes	Returns so good you can't wait to build more Popeyes

FIGURE 1: Roadmap to Results

FOCUS ON THE VITAL FEW

People think focus means saying yes to the thing you've got to focus on. But that's not what it means at all. It means saying no to the hundred other good ideas that there are. You have to pick carefully. I'm actually as proud of the things we haven't done as the things I have done.

STEVE JOBS, APPLE WORLDWIDE DEVELOPERS
CONFERENCE, MAY 13–16, 1997

After the first big global conference with franchisees, the Popeyes leadership team went back to the Atlanta headquarters and held our first meeting together. We were the team that was going to figure out *how* to get to the daring destination we had declared at the franchise meeting. In other words, we needed some concrete plans.

Having a strong belief that the people within the company always know what is wrong and what needs to be fixed, our first act was to schedule a meeting with the top leaders in the company: the directors, vice presidents, and the Popeyes leadership team. We went to a nearby conference center to focus on the work that needed to be done.

The people in the room identified the major issues facing the brand.

- Sales, guest transactions, and market share were declining.

- No pipeline of innovative new products existed to draw guests into the restaurant.

- No national media plan existed to tell the guests about Popeyes' great food.

- We had no compelling advertising message.

- Drive-thru speed of service was dead last in the ranking of quick-service chains.

- Guest ratings were great for our food and weak on virtually all other measures.

- Restaurants were tired and old-looking, in need of a remodel.

- Franchise owners were not making much money—and it was getting worse.

- New restaurants were opening but were performing poorly.

Other than that, things were going pretty well.

After the team had summarized the top problems that needed to be tackled at Popeyes, I put up a slide of all the current active projects at the company. There were 128. We were busy.

I drew this equation on the flip chart: Activity $\neq$ Results. Quiet in the room.

When I asked how long the issues facing the brand had existed, a veteran employee named Sondra raised her hand and said, "We put that list up on the wall every year at the off-site meeting."

After I absorbed the implication of her feedback, I asked her, "Would you like to be on the team that actually solves those issues?"

Without missing a beat, she responded, "Oh, yes, I would!"

Of course she would. How can your team be motivated and excited to contribute to the future if they know they are not working on the few vital matters that will lead to superior results?

The Dare-to-Serve leader must have the courage to focus on and solve the hard things facing the organization. We cannot serve the people well if we lead them through a long list of activities that don't change the performance of the organization. Instead, dare to act on the few game-changing initiatives that will deliver superior performance results.

WHY NOT FIX IT?

Why do leaders resist fixing the hard stuff that stands between mediocre and superior performance?

- Fear of failure?

- Absence of ideas?

- Worries about resources?

- Lack of courage?

I don't know. This I do know: A leader who is unwilling to tackle the real problems and fix them cripples the organization. If the team is not working on the real problems, they often make up work to justify their existence. They sense that their activities will not yield superior results. They become discouraged by the futility of it all. They hide at their desks and await the next round of bad news.

This was the mind-set of Popeyes. We were doomed if we stayed on the current course.

DARE-TO-SERVE REFLECTION #7 *What are the few vital things that must be addressed in your organization to drive better performance?*

As the leader, you have followers who are looking for your weaknesses and praying for your strengths. Give them what they pray for—a daring, aspirational plan that fixes real problems and yields results.

COMMIT THE RESOURCES

Unless such commitment is made,
there are only promises and hopes, but no plan.
PETER DRUCKER, DRUCKER MANAGEMENT

One of the questions followers have for a leader is, Will you put your money where your mouth is? Unfortunately for the people, leaders too often craft bold ambitions without providing resources for the organization to accomplish the vision.

When a leader commits sufficient resources to reach the daring destination, it conveys conviction, determination, and dedication to the goals. This may be the most important test of your leadership, from the followers' point of view.

The Popeyes franchisees taught us a lesson on this that we never forgot.

The leadership team and the ten elected franchise leaders of the Popeyes International Franchising Association—called the PIFA board—met at a Chicago airport hotel. Stuffed in a bad basement conference room, we were planning to ask our franchisees to shift our television advertising from 100 percent locally purchased programming to 100 percent nationally purchased cable programming. It was a bold, unprecedented request. If we accomplished it, Popeyes' message would reach twice as many people.

Our thesis was that national advertising would be the most effective way to accelerate awareness of the Popeyes brand and to encourage more people to eat at our restaurants. The challenge for the franchise owners was that we were asking them to let go of their franchisee-controlled media dollars behind local promotions for the benefit of the system as a whole.

The meeting began with an expert. A media guru spoke and provided an analysis of what Popeyes' television dollars would buy if we shifted local dollars to national television. This gentleman made the case that Popeyes was at a tipping point and that now was the perfect time for shifting to national media.

We expected the franchisees to be highly skeptical of the analysis, but the expert did his job well. He didn't try to put anything over on his audience. He had the facts in hand and spoke in layman's terms. He appeared to have Popeyes' best interests in mind. The franchise owners found him credible.

Next, the Popeyes brand marketing leader presented the idea of three national flights (about nine weeks of advertising in the next twelve months). It was a big dollar commitment—about $12 million. It would require all of the media dollars we had available annually across the entire U.S. system. If it didn't work, we would have used up the entire fund, with nothing in reserve.

We didn't have much proof of concept; Popeyes' prior experiences with national media had been mixed. But the franchisees seemed to understand that we were in a dire situation. Our sales trend had been negative for a long time. Popeyes needed to act boldly to get sales moving positively again. We needed to take risks. This is something entrepreneurs understood all too well.

After our brand marketing leader presented the case, the franchisees asked the Popeyes leadership team to leave the room so that they could talk among themselves. We had no way to predict whether we were moving toward war or alliance. We hadn't worked together very long and didn't have a track record of results together. If we reached agreement on this idea, it would be the first bold step we took together.

The time we spent in the hotel hallway seemed like forever. We started talking about what we would do to change the franchise owners' minds if they told us no. We were working on plan B.

They finally called us back into the room and said, "If you're so confident in this action, let's go big." Then the surprise: "We don't think nine weeks of advertising is a bold enough plan. We propose thirty-one weeks of national advertising over the next sixteen months. We think we can convince the Popeyes system to commit to this if you (the Popeyes franchisor) agree to invest $6 million in the advertising fund. What do you think?"

It was a test. A test of our conviction behind the idea and of our confidence in the bold idea.

The idea they proposed—that the corporate entity, the franchisor, would kick in money to the advertising fund—was unheard of, at Popeyes or anywhere else.

In this business model, franchisees contribute 3 to 4 percent of their total sales to fund Popeyes advertising. The corporation doesn't add to the fund. A $6 million investment in media would have no near-term economic return to Popeyes shareholders and would reduce our earnings by a significant amount in the first year.

How daring were we feeling now?

With some trepidation, the leadership team pitched the idea to the Popeyes board of directors. The presentation was inspired, but the projected results were not a sure bet. We asked the board to take the risk with us and to approve this bold investment so that we could demonstrate our conviction to the Popeyes system.

DARE-TO-SERVE REFLECTION #8 *Have you committed the resources needed to reach the daring destination?*

This decision proved to be a true turning point for Popeyes. The corporation made the big investment. The franchisees made the big commitment to move to national advertising. At first, the execution of the plan was imperfect. Fortunately, the following year, Popeyes restaurant guest traffic was positive for the first time in seven years. Total sales grew as well.

Years later, the franchisees would say that this one decision started the Popeyes brand on a multiyear trajectory of industry-leading performance. They were right. We made a bold decision together; we both took big risks. We put our money where our mouth was, and the strategy won in the marketplace.

BRING OUT THE BEST IN PEOPLE

*So much of what we call management consists
in making it difficult for people to work.*
    PETER DRUCKER

Dare-to-Serve leaders create work environments that bring out the best in their people. If you have an under-performing team, the easy thing to do is to say, "I need new people." Frankly, that is what most leaders do—they fire the people they have and go get new ones.

If you ask the people what constrains their perfor-mance, it is usually not skills; it is the work environment established by the leader. The work environment can inspire boldness, innovation, and excellence, or it can strangle the capability and productivity of the people and the team.

This is the work of the leader: to create a work envi-ronment that yields superior results.

After determining the vital few, hard things that need-ed to be fixed at Popeyes, the leadership team held a sec-ond off-site retreat with the top leaders in the company. The purpose of this meeting was to build more effective teamwork across the departments.

We played a "game," facilitated by a consultant, to teach us how teamwork drives performance. It was a production-line exercise in which groups competed to assemble and decorate an origami paper star called a Starship.

Three teams competed in the exercise. Team 2 was particularly inept at this game, and after three rounds of competition had not produced a single Starship that passed the quality assurance inspection. At this point, teams 1 and 3 were laughing at the dysfunction of team 2. Team 2 asked for a fifteen-minute huddle to reorganize their approach to the game.

When team 2 returned, their next round of production generated thirty-six Starships, and 100 percent of these passed the quality assurance inspection. This was more than twice the number of Starships produced by either of the other two teams. The room was stunned at the change in team 2's performance. Curiosity replaced laughter.

We asked team 2 to explain what had changed the trajectory of their performance. How did they go from laughable to laudable results? They said, "In the first rounds, we just put everyone in a job and basically said, 'Go fast.' Then we saw that we had multiple breakdowns. Bottlenecks caused by skill gaps and poor processes. We had people folding paper who couldn't fold paper. We had people coloring Starships who couldn't color. We had people on the sidelines watching but not contributing. We had high achievers cheering but not helping. We were dysfunctional."

"What did you do in the fifteen-minute break?" I asked.

"We asked people what position they thought they were best suited to, and then we placed them in that job. We had the process people reengineer our process. We had the artistic people color. We had people who folded paper best, fold the paper. We had enthusiastic coaches be enthusiastic coaches. We had timekeepers keep track of time. We encouraged one another and set a bold goal of beating the other two teams. Then we came back to the room and did our best work yet."

The Starship exercise revealed some remarkably simple lessons in leading high-performance teams:

- Find out the strengths of each team member and assign each to a role that uses those strengths.

- Determine the skill gaps on the team and add that capability to the team.

- Respect different talents in the team; everyone has something to contribute.

- Create both the processes and the environment for success.

- The leaders can't create winning results on their own. The team creates the win.

In capturing the lessons of this high-performing team 2, we decided to make this the new way of working together at Popeyes. We would build a cross-functional team approach to each business strategy on the Roadmap to Results. We would call the teams "Starship teams."

Here's how the teams were organized: Each team had an executive sponsor, a leadership team member who was available for coaching but was not directly involved in leading the team. The teams could seek out any talent they needed from any department in the company—in fact, cross-functional team members were a requirement. Each team chose a process person—called a project management officer—to ensure they had a work plan, milestones, and measurable results. Each team leader was coached on how to get the best work from his or her team in a collaborative fashion.

Interestingly, the real-world experiment with Starship teams had many of the same outcomes as the Starship game at the off-site meeting. We had teams that raced forward with some initial success but then stalled and had to regroup. We had teams that were completely dysfunctional at the start and then, by realizing their thought errors and making corrections, were able to outperform all the other teams. We had the steady teams that didn't set the world on fire with results at the start but then, as they grew together as a team, produced better and better outcomes.

Here are the results of the four high-performing Starship teams.

The Build a Distinctive Brand team reinvented the process for new product innovation. They created a research approach that steadily improved the success rate of new items in test markets. They expanded their team to include the most innovative franchise owners with a passion for superior food. In their third year together, the new products conceived by this team led to industry-leading sales results, and Popeyes won a *Nation's Restaurant News* MenuMasters Award for launching the year's most innovative new limited-time offer in quick-service restaurants.

The Run Great Restaurants team tackled Popeyes' slow speed of service. They studied the best-in-class competitors and determined that we needed new equipment, new processes, and retraining of our restaurant teams. They created a way to measure progress so we could see results. This team conducted an initial test in one restaurant to see whether they had a plan that worked. Then they expanded the test to a few markets to work out the details. When they launched the speed-of-service initiative nationally, with new equipment and retrained restaurant teams, we reached our speed goal of 75 percent of restaurants with an average drive-thru speed of 180 seconds or less, in one year. Before this initiative, we had been ranked dead last among our competitors on speed. Two years later we were featured in a leading industry publication as the competitor most focused on improved speed of service.

The Grow Restaurant Profits team chased cost savings in the supply chain, with a goal of saving the system a total of $7 million to $10 million, which was about half of a margin point on a restaurant profit and loss (P&L) statement. The team set up a process to examine every segment of the supply chain. They updated product specifications and rebid items to gain better pricing. They surveyed suppliers for savings ideas that would not degrade food quality and compiled a list of ideas with merit. They audited distribution centers and the purchasing processes to make sure cost errors were discovered and fixed. At the end of three years, this team had saved the restaurants more than $40 million, adding two full margin points to an average restaurant P&L.

The Accelerate Quality Restaurants team had the most difficult goal: to become an industry leader of new restaurant builds, with high volumes and high returns for the owners who would invest in them. At first it was difficult for this team to be successful, because the other three teams had to improve our current restaurant performance before the franchise owners would be excited about building *new* Popeyes restaurants.

As the saying goes, this team focused on what they could control. They purchased new site-selection software that immediately helped direct owners to better real estate with strong opening sales performance. This virtually eliminated the "dogs," the high failure rate of our prior new openings.

Using predictive software, the team mapped the top eleven market opportunities so that they could guide owners and resources to the best locations. They redesigned the materials we used to "sell" owners on the new build opportunity, highlighting the exciting returns on investment that the new restaurants were delivering. In 2016, the last year of our leadership, Popeyes built more quick-service drive-thru restaurants in the United States than any chain except McDonald's.

DARE-TO-SERVE REFLECTION #9 *What steps have you taken to create a work environment that brings out the best performance from your team?*

Not every team was as successful as these four. We had three teams that struggled to reach their goals or that decided to delay, based on new learning. There were no regrets and no failures. This fresh, new way of working produced an exciting, focused workplace where people across the company could contribute their skills to help deliver superior performance. It created an atmosphere that inspired new solutions and improved performance results.

This new way of working also had an unexpected benefit. It produced a cadre of new, high-performing leaders throughout the organization. We now had more opportunities for leaders to contribute and to grow in capability. We included a wider range of leaders in the teams. We gained visibility for our leaders, observing both their competencies and their character traits. Many of the leaders that we "discovered" in this process were promoted to greater responsibilities.

This better working environment stimulated people to grow and contribute their best work. It led to a new level of performance.

THE COURAGE TO MEASURE PROGRESS

You move what you measure.
POPEYES MANTRA

The lack of decision-making information available at Popeyes when I joined the company was startling. Essentially, we tracked dollar sales because that was the basis for collecting royalty payments from our franchise owners. We also had strong accounting processes for public-company reporting. Beyond that, we were clueless about the key metrics of the business.

As a result, we had many *passionate* conversations with our franchise owners. Virtually none of those conversations could be corroborated with facts.

We argued about whether our speed of service was as bad as we thought it was. We argued about whether restaurant profits were improving or not. We argued about whether marketing events were successes or failures.

Without data, the truth was not evident. Worse yet, each of us could hide behind our own version of the truth.

The Popeyes leadership team decided to go get the data we needed to inform decision making and measure progress. We didn't know what the data would say. The situation could be better than we thought, or it could be much worse. If we were going to serve the people well, we needed to know exactly where we stood. This required courage, because the facts don't lie.

We continued tracking sales, and we added a new measure—market share, our percentage of the chicken quick-service restaurant dollar sales. Market share was an important addition because it told us whether we were gaining or losing position relative to the competition.

We decided to install equipment to measure speed of service at the drive-thru windows, and we began collecting the average speed of service every week, for every restaurant.

We designed and fielded our first-ever guest experience monitor—a survey that guests used to tell us how we were doing. Within six months, we had guest feedback from every restaurant in the system.

Our biggest data gap was measuring restaurant operating profits. We had profitability data on only a few dozen company-owned restaurants, but none from the franchisee-owned restaurants. When we began collecting individual restaurant P&L statements, it was delivered in disparate ways—from computer downloads, Excel spreadsheets, or even handwritten charts. We hired a newly minted college graduate to trudge through the files, clean up the data, and make summary tables that we could analyze. After two years, we finally had a meaningful set of data with which to track profitability progress and to analyze our business decisions. This was the single biggest hurdle we overcame. We could now evaluate our performance by the same measure the franchise owner used—restaurant operating profits.

We then started collecting data on the performance of new restaurants, tracking return on investment. The predictive software tool we had purchased reduced the failure rate of new restaurants by helping owners find better real estate sites. The financial tracking data proved that those new restaurants were now achieving better return.

DARE-TO-SERVE REFLECTION #10 *What are the milestones and measurements of progress in your organization? Are you acting on what you learn from the data?*

The most courageous aspect of collecting this new data was the decision to report the data publicly to our employees, our franchise owners, our board, and our shareholders. We made a commitment that we would share the results, good or bad.

What was so important about establishing these new measures of performance?

- The numbers don't lie. Once you actually know the truth, you can start improving.

- The numbers don't lie. The numbers hold you accountable to making real improvements.

- The numbers don't lie. The numbers inspire you to make action plans for reaching goals.

Take note: measurements matter only if you plan to *act* upon what you learn. At Popeyes, we established routines to look at the data regularly and to adjust our plans if we fell short of the goals.

This sounds really basic. However, measuring progress, reporting results, and adjusting to the feedback was essential to improving Popeyes' performance. Measures held the team accountable for progress. Leadership is being courageous enough to measure and report performance results—to be accountable. This attention to accountability improves the odds of superior results.

PLAUSIBILITY OF THE GOALS

One potential thought error to watch out for with the daring destination is *plausibility*. The destination and goals that you set for the team, while challenging them to stretch and grow, must be achievable.

At Popeyes, one of the ways we determined the future state of the enterprise was to study our best competitors carefully. What sales and profit levels did they achieve? What guest satisfaction scores represented best in class? What level of restaurant operating profit was above average yet reachable?

This process of testing our daring aspirations to be sure they could be achieved was a critical step. If the destination had been hopelessly unrealistic, the team would not have believed in it. They would have held back their best work until there was evidence that this turnaround was real. Instead, they heard the business case behind the bold plan and they determined that success was *possible*.

Your team needs a clear understanding of how you define the daring destination—a business case that is compelling and gives them confidence to proceed.

WHAT IS THE DARING DESTINATION?—SUPERIOR RESULTS

When we started with the daring destination for Popeyes, we had no idea if we would be successful. Looking back, the performance results were stunning (see Table 2). We led the organization to eight years of growth in market share and sales. We had faster service at our drive-thrus. Restaurant profits and new restaurant returns were in the top tier of our industry.

No other quick-service restaurant delivered comparable results during this time frame. In fact, our primary chicken competitor experienced significant declines in sales, restaurant profits, and total number of restaurants in the United States during this time.

TABLE 2: Popeyes Performance Results

Average restaurant performance

	2008	2016	Results
Restaurant sales ($ millions)	1.0	1.45	Exceeded goal
Share of chicken quick-service (%)	14	24	Exceeded goal
Speed of service at drive-thru (seconds)	225+	180	Achieved
Restaurant operating profit (%)	18	23	Achieved
New restaurant owner returns (%)	< 10	≈ 25	Achieved

In 2016, we reached the daring destination we had defined back in 2007. Popeyes franchise owners were well served by these business results. The improved performance of the restaurants built owners' confidence in Popeyes' future. As such, the franchise owners chose to invest in that future by remodeling the existing restaurants and building new restaurants at a rapid pace.

DARING AND SERVING GO TOGETHER

Dare-to-Serve leaders challenge their followers with bold, courageous, exciting aspirations. The daring destination is designed to benefit the people and the enterprise, not just the leader.

The destination is a compelling, strategic road map with specific goals and action plans. It is focused on the vital few things that will drive superior performance. It has measurements and milestones to track progress, which are reported to the public.

The Dare-to-Serve leader creates an environment in which the people grow while pursuing the daring aspiration, gaining new confidence and valuable skills. On the way to the destination, the people are drawn together as an effective team. This leads to the desired outcome of a team performing at the highest level, driving results that cannot be produced by the leader alone.

With the courage of the dare—and the humility of the leader—daring destinations serve the people well.

THREE

WHY DO WE DO THIS WORK?

Most of us . . . have jobs that are too small for our spirits.
STUDS TERKEL, *WORKING*

WHY DOES WORK have such a bad reputation? Or is it just my line of work that has a bad reputation?

When you work in the restaurant business, you take a lot of flak for your job—particularly if you work in "fast food." Popular culture is full of unflattering references, such as "burger flipper" and "minimum-wage worker." Despite the fact that one in ten Americans currently works in a restaurant, one-third of Americans find their first job in a restaurant, and 50 percent of Americans work in a restaurant at some point in their working lives, restaurant work is regarded with disdain.

This drives me crazy. I know amazing people who work in the restaurant business. They deserve respect and dignity for what they do for a living. They feed people. They develop leaders. They help kids get through high school. They give people first and second chances for employment. They serve people kindly. They teach and counsel team members. They create jobs. They give generously in the community. They give the best of themselves to the people and the communities they serve.

Could we acknowledge and appreciate the purposeful, meaningful, valuable, and important work that restaurant people do?

Once I was visiting a top-performing restaurant manager in Chicago. She was full of positive energy for her work, and I asked her, "What is it that you love about this job?" She smiled and said, "Cheryl, I have the best job ever. I am a teacher, a counselor, a social worker, a mom, a minister, a finance advisor, and more. You see, in this position, I have the opportunity to impact the lives of young people just starting out. I help them get their grades up so that they can go to college. I teach them job skills so they can pay their bills. I help them solve problems when they don't have friends or family to help. I can't imagine a more important job in this community." For this restaurant manager, work has meaning and purpose.

Consider this thought: *It is the leader's responsibility to bring purpose and meaning to the work of the organization.*

Purpose and meaning are essential to creating a high-performance organization. When people believe their work matters, they contribute differently. They arrive early and stay late. They find creative solutions to problems. They build their skills so they can add more value. They work collaboratively to ensure the success of the team. They stay in the job longer.

Purpose and meaning at work raise the energy level, commitment, and performance of the team.

WHY DOES MEANING MATTER?

The Gallup organization publishes a study each year called *State of the American Workplace: Employee Engagement Insights for U.S. Business Leaders.* The most recent study, released in February 2017, states that 30 percent of the U.S. workforce is engaged in its work. Of course, this means that 70 percent of the workforce is not engaged in its work. More than twice as many people are "checked out" as are "checked in."

It should scare us to realize that only 21 percent of employees say that their performance is managed in a way that motivates them to do outstanding work. This fact alone should compel you to take action. If you want to see superior performance results, you must create an exceptional workplace of highly motivated people. The Gallup report says, "Know that every interaction with an employee has the potential to influence engagement and inspire discretionary effort."

Gallup's study goes on to explain that the highest-engagement companies, with 70 percent engaged employees, have significantly higher productivity, profitability, and customer ratings and less employee turnover. Gallup estimates that actively disengaged employees cost the U.S. economy $450 billion to $550 billion per year.

I've been reading this study every year it has been published since the year 2000. The statistics haven't changed much. The only thing I can conclude is that *leaders* haven't changed much.

What can a leader do to drive engagement? Help people find purpose and meaning at work. Inspire them to contribute their very best work. Care about them, so that they want to care about the enterprise. Until you do, the people are just biding their time, paying their bills, and waiting for something better to come along.

THE WORK THAT WE DO

As part of the turnaround of Popeyes, we decided that the organization should have clarity about the purpose of the work we do. Our leadership team came together, looked at our experiences in this industry, reviewed the values and beliefs we have about restaurant careers, and thought about the role we have in developing leaders.

The conversation started with these beliefs:

> We were proud of the career paths our industry offers. Many Popeyes franchise owners began as a fry cook or front counter person and became successful entrepreneurs owning multiple restaurants. Many of the restaurant general managers started at the front counter, later running a restaurant business with sales of more than $1.5 million annually. We developed leaders in this business—and we celebrated that fact.

> We were proud of the quality of food that our teams prepared for our guests each day. We were proud of the training that we offered, to teach people good work habits, food sanitation skills, teamwork, and problem solving. We were proud that we earned our living serving other people—our owners, our team members, our guests. We were proud of the opportunities we brought to developing countries around the globe. We were in the service industry—and we celebrated that fact.

This discussion led us to declare the *purpose* of our work at Popeyes: *Inspire servant leaders to achieve superior results.*

We decided that servant leadership would be our philosophy. We were in the business of serving others a delicious meal. Why not lead from the same vantage point?

Servant leadership simply means *service above self.* We decided to serve others well.

Superior results are the measure of how well we serve. Serving and performing go hand in hand.

We created the Popeyes purpose in the fall of 2011, nearly three years after we had begun the turnaround of the company. Why did we choose that time?

The turnaround was well under way. We had begun to experience some success in the bold, ambitious goals we had set for the enterprise. We were serving our franchise owners well, but we were not sure that the success would continue. We worried that we would be just another "one-hit wonder" leadership team who came together for a few years and generated good results and then went our separate ways. What could we do to lead the organization to sustainable success?

While we believed that the work we were doing was purposeful, we weren't sure that the rest of the organization shared our conviction. Maybe it was purposeful for us but "just a job" for them.

We analyzed what we had done well and what we needed to do next. We realized that we had not explained to our followers why the work we were doing was important, why we passionately believed in the future of Popeyes. The organization as a whole needed to share in that purpose. At the very next company meeting, we revealed our newly crafted Popeyes purpose to the team:

The Popeyes purpose: Inspire servant leaders to achieve superior results.

THE PLAQUE PROBLEM

The Popeyes purpose was well received by the people. We had to spend a fair amount of time explaining servant leadership, helping people to understand that it simply meant service to others above self. Other than that, people seemed to understand the purpose. They thought it was laudable. I'm not sure what they said privately after the meeting. I suspect it was something like, "Let's see if this purpose really changes the way we work at Popeyes."

We ran into what every company runs into. Purpose statements are nice. A few people get excited about them and live them in their daily work. Most people leave them right where they saw them—on the plaque on the wall.

Plaques hang on walls. Plaques collect dust. Plaques don't drive superior performance results.

Popeyes people weren't against the purpose; they just had no personal connection to the statement.

I began to challenge the leaders of the company in one-on-one meetings and in large groups. I said, "That purpose statement is a plaque at Popeyes. It hangs on the wall. Alone, it has no meaning and no impact on performance. The only Popeyes purpose anyone ever meets is *your* purpose."

No one ever met a plaque. No one ever gave a plaque credit for inspiring them to serve, for helping them reach their potential, or for driving superior results. Plaques don't do that. *People do.*

JOURNEY TO PERSONAL PURPOSE

[Work] is about a search . . . for daily meaning
as well as daily bread.

STUDS TERKEL, *WORKING*

At Popeyes, we conducted an experiment to determine whether purpose drives performance. We asked each Popeyes team member to develop a personal purpose. The process begins with a workshop we call Journey to Personal Purpose.

During a one-day session, a facilitator took the participants through a series of exercises to help them discover their core motivation—a *purpose* that gave their work meaning beyond the paycheck. The class started with an overview of the Popeyes purpose, sharing perspective on what servant leadership is and why we believe it is the most powerful path to superior performance results.

Then the class got personal.

Journey to Personal Purpose Exercise 1: Life Line

The leader asked team members to draw a time line of the significant events in their lives that shaped who they are as a leader, identifying three to five seminal moments, events, or experiences that shaped their approach to work and leadership.

Perhaps they were a middle child or the "baby" in the family, and this birth order contributed to who they are and how they approach leadership.

Perhaps there was a traumatic event in their life—the loss of a parent, an illness, an accident—that sent them in a new direction, good or bad, and profoundly shaped their view of the world and of work.

Perhaps there were certain people who mentored them—a teacher, an uncle, a manager at their first job—people who taught them important things that they want to evidence in their work and leadership.

Perhaps they had a difficult job or boss at an early age and that shaped who they want to be as a leader.

Each participant filled in his or her "life line" chart with three to five key events, and then they shared their life line with a small group. At most workshops, this conversation was full of genuine emotion as the participants shared those life experiences that fundamentally defined who they are.

DARE-TO-SERVE REFLECTION #11 *How well do you know the people who work for you? Do you know the three or four events in their lives that have shaped who they are today?*

Journey to Personal Purpose Exercise 2: Values Clarification

The second activity was a card game to help prioritize the most important values and beliefs that people bring to the workplace and to leadership. For this exercise, we used a deck of cards from the John Maxwell Company that lists thirty-four values, with a one-sentence definition of each. The deck includes blank cards, allowing participants to add a value if they don't find one of their most important values in the stack.

Individuals started by picking their top ten priority values. Then they studied that stack of ten cards and chose the three values that are most important at work. This process was a real struggle for people. They always asked, "Do I have to narrow the list to three values?"

The class facilitator told them that if either family or faith/religion was a top value, they could set those off to the side—know that they are high importance but focus their efforts on selecting the next three values that they want to evidence at work.

This step seemed to magically focus people on their top three values for work and leadership.

Why is this exercise so important? We all have values, beliefs, and convictions. Yet few people can articulate their top-priority values when asked. Too often, we speak in generalities, saying words that we think others want to hear. We want to be thought of as honest, genuine, trustworthy, and about thirty other things. But when we are honest with ourselves, we aren't really focused on any particular value at work. We are simply attempting to be good people, doing the best that we can.

As a leader, knowing the values of your team members helps you understand their convictions and their motivations. This understanding leads to more open conversations and less conflict and misunderstanding.

DARE-TO-SERVE REFLECTION #12 *If you knew the top-priority values of the people on your team, how would you lead more effectively?*

Journey to Personal Purpose Exercise 3: StandOut Roles

The third activity in a Journey to Personal Purpose workshop was a process to discover, uncover, and celebrate the talents of each person. For this exercise we used an online assessment tool called StandOut, created by author and researcher Marcus Buckingham. The assessment determines the primary and secondary roles where the participants' talents and skills are maximized. The report makes them aware of the ways they can best contribute at work and gives them tips on how to use these strengths to their advantage.

DARE-TO-SERVE REFLECTION #13 *Most leaders can tell you the weaknesses of their team members. But can you cite the strengths and talents of your team? Are you accessing their very best capability?*

At Popeyes, we believed that every individual is uniquely designed with strengths that they bring to the workplace. If people do not know their own talents and their leader doesn't know them either, we cannot put people in a position for success. As I often remark, "I must know you to grow you."

StandOut roles are a person's "superpowers," the best traits they can contribute to the team. We asked each person to think about how their talents support their personal purpose. We wanted them to bring their best capabilities to the table to help drive superior performance.

Journey to Personal Purpose Exercise 4: Personal Purpose

After completing these three exercises—assessing life experiences, values, and strengths—we took team members through a process to craft their personal purpose for work as shown in Figure 2. This is the statement, in one or two sentences, that describes why they come to work each day and how they will positively impact the organization.

The personal purpose statement answers these inquiries:

Throughout my life and work experience, I've discovered these key themes . . .

My top three values are . . .

My StandOut strengths are . . .

My personal purpose for leadership is . . .

My purpose can serve the organization by . . .

Very few people got their purpose done by the end of the workshop. Most wanted to let it simmer for a few days, weeks, or months, checking to make sure it had real meaning—they wanted a purpose that would make a difference in work and leadership. This takes time, as it should. It is too important to rush.

DARE-TO-SERVE REFLECTION #14 *What would happen if you helped your team discover and pursue their personal purpose? How would they contribute differently to the performance of the team?*

Personal **Purpose**

Throughout my life/work experience
I've discovered these key themes:

- _____
- _____
- _____

My top three values:

- _____
- _____
- _____

My StandOut strengths:

- _____
- _____
- _____

My personal purpose for leadership is:

_____

_____

_____

_____

My purpose can serve the organization by:

_____

_____

_____

_____

FIGURE 2: The Personal Purpose Statement

Your role as a leader is to encourage team members to complete their statements, sharing your own perspective on how meaningful purpose has been to you. Let them know you are looking forward to talking about their personal purpose. This tells them you are interested in them and value their contributions.

The Journey to Personal Purpose exercise and instructions can be found at www.cherylbachelder.com.

THE IMPACT OF PERSONAL PURPOSE

When a team member landed on their personal purpose, it helped them determine how they connect with the Popeyes purpose. How would they inspire servant leaders to achieve superior results? What follows are several personal purpose statements from Popeyes leaders. They are diverse and distinctly personal. In every case, their personal purpose had a positive impact on the performance of Popeyes.

"My purpose is to unleash each individual's unique gift to drive innovation." Dick led a team of creative people. Creative people can be a challenge to lead—each person a different personality, each a bit sensitive to criticism. Dick's job was to bring out of this team inspired, innovative ideas for Popeyes, such as new menu items, new packaging, new seating designs, and new advertising. This talented team identified, explored, and executed bold new ideas to grow sales for Popeyes. Dick's personal purpose "unleashed" industry-leading innovation for Popeyes because of his passion for creating an environment where creative people thrive.

"My purpose is to inspire others to build positive, healthy relationships to better serve the community." Alice had responsibility for overseeing the supply chain and quality assurance functions. In this role, she led teams to seek fresh, innovative solutions for a host of Popeyes challenges. Alice loved to solve problems in teams. She created an award called the Can-Do Award to celebrate people who built positive relationships that helped solve Popeyes problems. Her purpose helped us access more than $40 million in savings for the Popeyes system, which significantly improved profit margins at the restaurants.

"My purpose is to create safe work environments where people can take risks and grow to their full potential." Andrew's life line reminded him that he has worked in some toxic environments over the years—places that discouraged him and inhibited the performance of the team. Andrew decided to be a different kind of leader, a leader who provided a healthy environment for taking risks and learning new things. The atmosphere in his department was a lovely combination of high expectations and encouraging words. The people stretched and took risks and grew in capability. Once Andrew arrived at Popeyes, the performance results of his team accelerated. I don't think this is a coincidence.

"My purpose is to inspire others to know that it's never too late to live, to love, to matter." ZR's early life was not easy. He witnessed injustice and discrimination in the life of his grandfather. He experienced tragedy when his mother was killed. He struggled with navigating life and work. But instead of declaring defeat, ZR declared victory. He served as vice president of operations at Popeyes. He

determined that his top three values were *sacrifice* (it's not about me), *timing* (it's never too late), and *redemption* (grace and forgiveness). These values led him to the conclusion that every person deserves to be left whole, no matter what their circumstances. ZR's personal purpose is to inspire those with difficult starts in life—it is never too late to live, to love, to matter. The impact? He was a beloved coach in our restaurants.

"My purpose is to inspire others to passionately share and pursue their big ideas." Kelsey grew up as a middle child in a family of six children in a small town called Highlands, North Carolina. Kelsey's ideas and ambitions were bigger than her town, and when she graduated from high school, she moved to the city and began pursuing those dreams. Looking back, Kelsey remembered that it was hard to find her voice and confidence from that middle-child position. When she served as Popeyes' internal communications leader, she encouraged and supported people with big ideas. Through her work, she gave voice to the big ideas we were making happen at Popeyes.

Each person who discovers and applies his or her unique personal purpose brings the best of themselves to work. Through the personal purpose process, people better understood how they connected to the purpose of Popeyes. That led them to contribute more intentionally to the performance of Popeyes.

SHARING PERSONAL PURPOSE

After a team member developed a personal purpose, the first thing the supervisor encouraged him or her to do was to share it with others. This proved to be critical.

When one shares one's personal purpose with others, these benefits occur:

1. They receive positive feedback, encouragement, and suggestions from people who have worked side by side with them. This helps confirm and polish the purpose so that it is genuine and actionable.

2. Their coworkers gain a deeper understanding of who they are and how they best contribute at work. As a result, the coworkers know when to ask for their help and contribution to the team.

3. They gain support from their coworkers. A personal purpose helps the team know a person's strengths and motivations. In turn, the team becomes that person's *advocate* more often than becoming their critic.

4. They feel a part of something greater than themselves and accountable for contributing their best.

ACTING ON PERSONAL PURPOSE

A personal purpose is just a piece of paper until it is put into action in daily life. At Popeyes, the leaders who had an action plan for their personal purpose had more impact on the business. We found that the best practice was to have team members bring their personal purpose action plan to their annual and midyear performance reviews. These are good times to review their purpose, encourage them to put it into action, and discuss specific ways to act on the purpose in the upcoming months.

Dare-to-Serve leaders help their followers discover their personal purpose. This builds intentionality and engagement and leads to positive outcomes, including superior results.

Don't believe me. Ask around. Find a few people who have a well-defined personal purpose. Then look at their contribution to the team and the enterprise. Look at their results. It is no accident.

Personal purpose leads to sustained superior performance. When you know why you come to work, you show up differently. You are more intentional in what you do. You care more about the outcomes. You give your best efforts. This is what the concept of "highly engaged" looks like at work.

DISCOVERING WHY WE WORK BRINGS SUPERIOR RESULTS

At Popeyes, we measured employee engagement to discover the personal connection of our people to the enterprise. There are many drivers of team member engagement; personal purpose is only one of them. Nonetheless, I would say that the Popeyes Employee Engagement Index was the best indicator we had to measure the impact of personal purpose on performance.

Using an independent research firm that is expert in measuring employee engagement, Popeyes conducted an annual study. The Popeyes Employee Engagement Index was a statistical compilation of responses to these four statements:

I am proud to work for Popeyes.

I rarely think about looking for a new job with another company.

I would recommend Popeyes as a great place to work.

Overall, I am extremely satisfied with Popeyes as a place to work.

In 2012, the research firm reported that Popeyes' overall Employee Engagement Index of 78 percent was significantly above the norm of 69 percent for their other client companies. The top 25 percent of Popeyes leaders, those with the highest engagement index scores, excelled at 89 percent. These indexes were derived from "top two box" scores, meaning ratings of 4 or 5 on a five-point scale.

We continued to measure employee engagement each year, expanding the survey to include employees in the restaurants. In 2016, we surveyed nearly 35,000 employees. Using the higher bar metric of "top box" engagement (a rating of 5 on a five-point scale), Popeyes' employee engagement was 45 percent, compared to a norm of 29 percent as shown in Table 3. These significantly above-average scores for employee engagement are concrete evidence of the strong culture we built at Popeyes.

TABLE 3: Popeyes Engagement Results

	Total Popeyes (%)	Industry Norm (%)
2016 Popeyes Employee Engagement Index	45	29

HELP THOSE WHO WANT TO BE HELPED

At Popeyes, we found that personal purpose makes a difference for the organization. Personal purpose clarifies where the people stand and unleashes their talent.

Even so, we could only help those who wanted to be helped. Personal purpose is only effective for those who *want* to have purpose and meaning in their life. It is not for everybody. Many people go through life without a personal purpose—and they don't mind at all.

We had several leaders opt out of the Journey to Personal Purpose. And we let them. This problem takes care of itself over time. Those who have no clear personal purpose are not highly engaged and typically do not contribute their best work. Eventually, they leave or are asked to leave the organization. And the organization becomes stronger.

Helping people who want to find meaning and purpose at work is exceptionally rewarding. It is the leader's opportunity to leave a legacy in the lives of the people you lead.

Personal purpose accelerates employee engagement and the performance of the organization.

FOUR

HOW WILL WE **WORK TOGETHER**?

Alone we can do so little; together we can do so much.
HELEN KELLER

THE TURNAROUND OF A TEAM'S performance or a company's performance requires a compelling strategic plan—a road map that gives clarity about *what* the team or company will do to get to the daring destination we talked about in chapter 2. This well-defined business plan is essential to helping an organization grow. Without it, the team will fail.

A strategic road map is *essential*, but it is *insufficient* to drive superior results.

As important as *what* you decide to do is to decide *how* you will work together to accomplish the plan. What principles will guide the daily work of the team, enabling them to serve one another, and the business plan, well? What principles, when put into action, will lead to superior results?

Some call this the *culture* of the organization, which is a good word for it, because it means the way we think, behave, and work together to accomplish goals. Defining the principles of the culture and holding the team accountable to those principles is fundamentally the work and the responsibility of the leader.

Done well, principles are the fuel for accelerating the team's performance. Without principles in action, the leader cannot drive superior results—and may, in fact, risk disaster.

DARE-TO-SERVE REFLECTION #15 *What are the principles of your organization? Are they evident in the daily actions of the team members?*

The many ethical debacles in major corporations have increased my zeal for principled leadership. Enron Corporation claimed the four values of *respect, integrity, communication,* and *excellence* in its corporate documents and plaques. In a *New York Times* article, James Kunen quotes a person who commented on the reality of Enron's corporate values, saying, "Why not just come right out and say it? 'We will strive to make as much money as we can without going to prison.'"

For principles to matter, they have to be "in action," not on plaques. Principles must come alive in the daily conversations, decisions, and actions of the team.

POPEYES PRINCIPLES
At Popeyes, we chose six principles to help us work together as shown in Figure 3. These principles guided our daily actions and supported our purpose: to inspire servant leaders to achieve superior results.

We are passionate about what we do.

We listen carefully and learn continuously.

We are fact-based and planful.

We coach and develop our people.

We are personally accountable.

We value humility.

Far more important than the words on the plaque, however, is the *use* of these principles in our daily work. Let's look at examples of how we worked together at Popeyes, using these six principles.

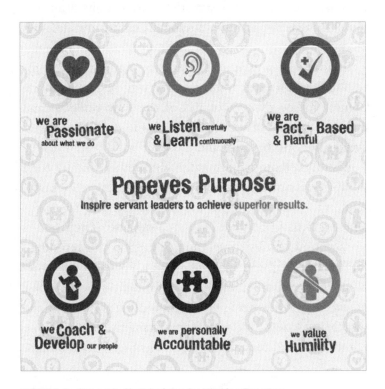

FIGURE 3: Popeye's Six Principles for Working Together

We are passionate about what we do

Nothing great was ever achieved without enthusiasm.
RALPH WALDO EMERSON, "*CIRCLES*"

At Popeyes, our first principle was "We are passionate about what we do." We didn't define the specifics of what passion looks like for you. We just wanted you to have it. As leaders, our passion was the fuel that inspired people to move toward a bold ambition for the organization.

We decided that this principle of passion was particularly important to a franchise organization. Popeyes franchisees have a lot of passion—and they should. They made a huge decision to invest in the Popeyes business; they are "all-in." As a result, they care deeply about the decisions that impact their business. That passion deserves respect.

In 2011, we presented to the system a new design for remodeling Popeyes restaurants. We took ten franchise owners to see the prototypes of the new building and dining room in New Orleans. We were excited to reveal the future look of the brand.

The franchise owners hated the new look. In their view, it was not contemporary enough. It cost too much. It didn't stand up well to the new designs of Starbucks and McDonald's. They were passionate. They had a strong point of view: they did not support this remodel.

The Popeyes leadership team was terribly disappointed in their response, and we were inclined to argue our point of view. Instead, we respected the passion of the franchise owners. We wanted the franchise leaders to be enthusiastic and committed to the new restaurant design, for they would inspire the whole Popeyes system to remodel. Lack of passion for the new design would doom the results of the remodel program.

DARE-TO-SERVE REFLECTION #16 *How is passion demonstrated in the daily actions of you and your team?*

We accepted the franchise owners' feedback. We started over on the design and two years later presented a contemporary, strong remodel design that the franchisees loved at first sight. The franchise owners' passion for this new look led our system to remodel 80 percent of the restaurants in a two-year period, a task that would typically have taken five or more years. Passion drove performance results.

Dare-to-Serve leaders welcome passion to the team. Passion is the fuel of the organization—it drives superior performance.

We listen carefully and learn continuously

Don't assume, because you are intelligent, able, and well-motivated, that you are open to communication, that you know how to listen.
ROBERT K. GREENLEAF, *SERVANT LEADERSHIP*

When my daughter Tracy was thirteen, she began behaving as most teenagers do. She broke the rules. She talked back. She slept late. She came home late. She left wet towels on the floor.

But her most annoying teenager behavior?

When I attempted to tell her something, she would put a finger in each ear to block the sound of my voice and say, "Mini headphones . . . Can't hear you . . ."

Somewhere along the way to adulthood, we tend to stop listening and learning from others. In fact, it's worse than that. As adults, we start telling everybody what to do—and we call it leadership.

Wrong answer.

What gets in the way of listening and learning? It's simple. As leaders, we want to think that we have all the answers. Having all the answers makes us feel indispensable to the organization and secure in our jobs.

Unfortunately, nothing could be further from the truth.

Andy Stanley, the leader of North Point Ministries, says it this way: "The leader's IQ declines with every promotion."

With every promotion, the leader gets further from the people, further from the facts, and further from the insights he or she needs to lead. Listening carefully and learning continuously are the antidote for our distance from reality.

At Popeyes, we chose "We listen carefully and learn continuously" as our second principle because we knew we would need frequent reminders to listen to the franchisees, and we knew we would need to learn from our mistakes.

For example, at one point we had a difficult matter come up about sourcing a particular product for our restaurants—a supply chain problem. There was a significant difference of opinion between the leaders of Popeyes and the franchise leaders who oversaw the Popeyes purchasing and distribution cooperative.

The Popeyes leadership team was mad about the matter.

When leaders get mad, listening and learning go out the window. Mad leaders know exactly what they want to say. They cut to the chase and tell you exactly how they feel—which is highly efficient but very ineffective. The unfortunate truth: efficiency with people ruins relationships.

Our leadership team caught ourselves going down the wrong path and reconsidered our principle. We envisioned the outcome of a "mad meeting," where everyone leaves with steam coming out of their ears and nothing is solved. We needed to choose a better path. We decided we would be less direct with our concerns at the beginning of the meeting. We would ask questions to clarify, and spend time listening carefully to the franchise owners' point of view.

DARE-TO-SERVE REFLECTION #17 *Are you and your team listening carefully and learning continuously from the people you serve?*

Our self-talk was saying, *How slow and inefficient.* Yet we chose to let the principle prevail: *Listen and learn.*

We opened the meeting with a friendly exchange. We asked open-ended questions to gather more information about the issue. We learned some things we did not know, that changed our understanding of the matter. We found the franchise owners to be more open to new ideas than we expected. They were willing to consider some new approaches to find a better solution together.

Over the course of a few days of follow-up conversations, the problem was resolved in a way that was acceptable to all parties. Listening and learning provided the path to a superior outcome for all.

It's not a natural instinct, but a Dare-to-Serve leader pauses—listens carefully and learns continuously—before taking action. Invariably, this helps the people reach alignment on the next steps so that they can execute them with excellence. This leads to a better outcome than a leader's unilateral decision.

We are fact-based and planful

There are abundant current examples of loss of leadership that stems from a failure to foresee what reasonably could have been foreseen, and from failure to act on that knowledge while the leader had freedom to act.

ROBERT K. GREENLEAF, *SERVANT LEADERSHIP*

You may be surprised to see a principle about being "fact-based and planful." It sounds more like a process for doing business than a principle. At Popeyes, we chose to make this a principle because it revolutionized the way we work. Better facts and better planning have built trust and alignment with the franchise owners. Perhaps we could have called this principle "collaborate," for that is the true benefit of being fact-based and planful—it enables collaboration.

As I mentioned earlier, at the beginning of the turn-around, we had no financial data on the performance of the restaurants. As a result, we didn't know whether the marketing promotions we used to drive sales were profit-able to the owners or not. We needed facts.

A year later, a veteran franchisee chastised our leader-ship team by saying that the June promotion had nearly bankrupted the Popeyes system because we discounted the core menu meals. I paused for a moment and then said calmly, "Actually, the Popeyes system had its high-est absolute dollar profits, in June, of any promotion in the past year." The franchise owner asked me how I knew that to be true. I said, "Because we have over one thousand restaurant P&Ls in hand." He smiled and said, "Then you actually know!"

Facts remove whim and personal opinion from the de-cision process. Over time, facts build trust, alignment, and effective collaboration with the people we serve. Planning has a similar effect.

DARE-TO-SERVE REFLECTION #18 *What process do you have for collecting and analyzing the facts? What process do you have for planning the future?*

We used to plan Popeyes marketing promotions from month to month, and we were in a constant cycle of meet-ings to pick the next promotion. It was exhausting, and our picks didn't perform very well. To correct this situation, we created a three-year planning process for promotions.

We built a promotion calendar that was organized by what sells in each season. We agreed on how many new products we needed each year, and they were tested and proven before launch. The calendar-planning meeting was highly organized, the promotions were chosen based on factual data, and our success rate improved dramatically.

Planning reduces last-minute decisions. Rushed decisions are often the wrong decisions.

The Dare-to-Serve leader gathers the facts needed for decision making and builds a planning process. In doing so, the leader builds trust, alignment, and collaboration with the people served. Over time, the better-considered decisions and more thoughtful plans lead to improved performance results.

We coach and develop our people

To put it simply and starkly: If you don't get the people process right, you will never fulfill the potential of your business.
LARRY BOSSIDY, RETIRED CEO OF ALLIED SIGNAL

When we chose this fourth principle at Popeyes—"We coach and develop our people"—it was for a different reason than all the others. Our study of servant leadership convinced us that coaching and developing people was a signature trait of a servant leader company, but it was not a core competency at Popeyes. Developing our people was, in general, an afterthought.

DARE-TO-SERVE REFLECTION #19 *What is your coaching routine? Do you have a specific and thoughtful development plan for each of your team members?*

We had good excuses. The restaurant business is 24/7. The leadership team worked long hours. We traveled from city to city, visiting restaurants and solving problems. When would we find time for coaching and developing people, other than during a once-a-year performance review?

In feedback sessions, people told us we that we had significant opportunities for growing, developing, and recognizing our people.

Our first step was to declare that developing great leaders was a central strategy for the enterprise. We then hired human resource professionals to develop effective people practices. We began to put resources behind this aspirational principle.

We began by setting performance objectives and preparing annual development plans for each person. We reviewed talent on a regular basis and looked for assignments to challenge top performers. We encouraged supervisors to have biweekly one-on-one coaching sessions with those who reported to them, to clarify expectations, ask coaching questions, and process decisions in a timely manner. We created a compelling leadership development program called Lead from the Heart to invest in our team members. It included a coaching process to help leaders advance this competency in the organization. We were beginning to roll this out to all leaders in the system in 2017.

We were at the early stages of improving our coaching and development practices. I share this with you to be completely transparent with the Popeyes story. We did some principles very well, but we still had a long way to go in this area. I believe if you have a principle that you know is critical to driving superior performance, you have to say so—even if you fall short on that principle today.

We were planning to become a company that was known for its leadership development because we had conviction about the principle of coaching and developing leaders. This principle held us accountable to drive change in our daily actions over time.

We are personally accountable

The price of greatness is responsibility.
WINSTON CHURCHILL

Each Popeyes principle had a visual symbol: a puzzle piece. We chose this symbol to communicate the importance of each person doing "their piece of the puzzle." That is what personal accountability looks like—a puzzle in which all the pieces lock together to form a picture.

We wanted Popeyes leaders and franchise owners to do what they said they were going to do, to live up to their promises. We wanted them to own the roles and responsibilities of their job. We wanted them to quickly fess up and ask forgiveness if they made a mistake. We wanted them to solve the problems they discovered, not deny responsibility or point fingers and blame.

This principle is inherently important in a franchisor–franchisee partnership. The business model would not work if either one of us were to shirk our accountabilities.

For example, when a franchisor lacks accountability for building the brand or the operating system, the franchisees' business suffers, and they cannot overcome the problem on their own. When a franchisee fails to treat guests well or to serve quality food, the franchisor and the brand are damaged and cannot overcome the issue without action on the franchise owner's part. The business was designed as a symbiotic relationship, a partnership. Accountability is required.

Other businesses may be structured differently, but every business requires collaboration among people to execute the business plan. I can't think of a business where one leader, acting alone, can deliver superior performance. We all operate in interdependent teams that rely on each team member or each department to do their piece of the puzzle.

DARE-TO-SERVE REFLECTION #20 *How do you hold your team accountable and discourage victim mind-sets or blaming others? How does your team hold you personally accountable?*

The Dare-to-Serve leader understands the critical importance of personal accountability in reaching superior performance.

We value humility

Ego can't sleep. It micro-manages. It disempowers.
It reduces our capability. It excels in control.
STEPHEN COVEY

At Popeyes, you would often hear this phrase: "If you say you are humble, you are not."

Humility is the toughest principle to talk about and the toughest principle to do. If you *talk* about humility, you might look as though you *think* you are humble. Your team will be quick to notice the examples of when you are not humble. If you aspire to *be* humble in your daily actions, you will struggle to be consistent. Your team will be quick to notice this as well.

When the Popeyes leadership team was developing the six principles for serving others, this principle was non-negotiable for all of us. It belonged on the plaque. We wanted humility to be evident in our daily actions.

Why? Our career experiences had yielded this common conclusion: Leaders without humility are hell to work for. They are concerned primarily with themselves. They rarely consider the views or needs of others.

DARE-TO-SERVE REFLECTION #21 *How do you and your team model humility in your daily actions?*

We agreed that we are not naturally humble, either. That means there were plenty of days we were hell to work for, too. Therefore, humility *must* be a principle that we have conviction about, or we will never demonstrate humility to our teams. This principle will forever be an aspiration, not an accomplishment. As hard as we try, we will repeatedly fall short.

Humble leaders inspire, but self-centered leaders squash the spirit of the people. Dare-to-Serve leaders *aspire* to be more humble.

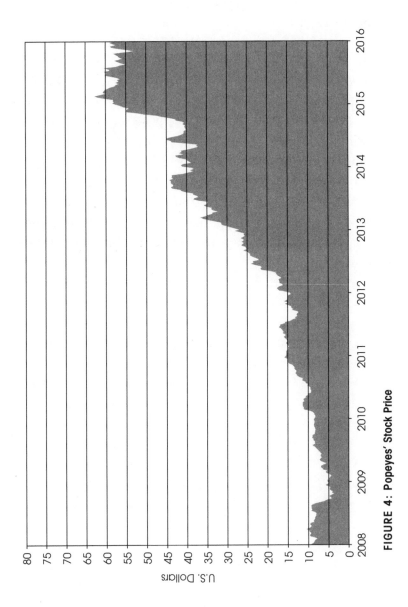

FIGURE 4: Popeyes' Stock Price

HOW WE WORK TOGETHER FOR SUPERIOR RESULTS

Does Dare-to-Serve leadership work? Does it drive superior results?

Financial performance is the bottom line for proving the case for Dare-to-Serve leadership—and we delivered the goods. Perhaps nothing is more stunning than Popeyes' share price performance. From February 2008 to December 2016, the Popeyes share price grew from $8.90 to $61.31, as indicated in Figure 4. The stock also outpaced the S&P 500 restaurant sector and the total S&P 500 during this time frame.

Wall Street, take note. While a compelling business strategy is essential, the principles that guide *how* leaders accomplish that plan will determine the trajectory of the results.

Principles perform.

FIVE

WHAT IS THE **LEGACY** OF THE **LEADER?**

Things might have been different,
but they could not have been better.

J. R. R. TOLKIEN, *LEAF BY NIGGLE*

ON TUESDAY, FEBRUARY 21, 2017, CNBC ran this headline: "Restaurant Brands in Deal to Acquire Popeyes Louisiana Kitchen for $1.8 billion." The deal announcement stated that Restaurant Brands International (RBI) would pay $79 a share in cash for Popeyes, "a 27 percent premium to Popeyes thirty-trading day volume weighted average price of February 10," the last trading day before the media got wind of the deal. Maxim Group stock analyst Stephen Anderson wrote in a research note, "We believe the Popeyes acquisition would provide Restaurant Brands a concept that provides steady organic and unit growth in both the North American and overseas markets."

RBI communicated its $79 offer to the Popeyes board of directors on Presidents' Day weekend of 2017. The board deliberated and deemed the proposal was in the best interest of the shareholders. I announced the decision to the franchisees and employees early Tuesday morning, February 21, and then the press release hit the

Associated Press wire. The closing would be in approximately thirty days.

This was an unexpected announcement for the franchisees and employees. The company was moving full throttle on Popeyes road map strategies. We had publicly disclosed a major technology initiative and an acceleration of international openings at the stock analyst day in the fall of 2016. But with the news of the sale, there would be a new owner, a new strategy, a new culture, and a new leadership team.

My tenure as CEO ended with the sale closing on March 27, 2017. That afternoon, the CEO of RBI, Daniel Schwartz, came to my office, shook my hand, and wished me well. I went to the People Services department and gave them my employee badge and office key and carried my box of photos and mementos out to the car. Nine years and five months from beginning to end.

One week later, I drove to Charlotte, North Carolina, to honor a long-standing commitment to speak at a leadership event for about one hundred executives from companies across the Southeast. I gave my prepared speech and then asked if there were any questions. The first question was "People say that the legacy of a leader is best expressed by what happens after they leave the role. How do you feel about your exit from Popeyes?"

I answered the question by saying, "A public-company board of directors hired me to lead Popeyes. I loved the Popeyes team and the results we created for the franchisees, but I was never the owner of the company. My work was in service to this organization. I am grateful to the board for giving me the opportunity to lead by the principles I believe drive superior performance. It has been an incredible capstone career experience. I rest well knowing that, for nearly ten years, this leadership team has served well. That will be our legacy."

More than a year has now passed since the sale of the company, and I have had time to rest and reflect on the experience. I've even had the wonderful opportunity to teach about the Popeyes transformation to a group of second-year MBA students at Indiana University, my alma mater. The process of preparing for this course reminded me of the essential elements of turning around an enterprise. For those of you needing to change the trajectory of your organization, here is a summary of the framework we used to lead a successful transformation at Popeyes.

1. LISTEN FIRST

Always listen first. We began the turnaround of Popeyes with a listening tour of seven cities—hearing from franchisees, restaurant managers, and guests. Every strategy we selected stemmed from what we learned on this trip. Over the next nine years, if we hit a bump in performance results, we went back out and listened again.

2. ARTICULATE A PURPOSE: "WHY"

Simon Sinek's popular book tells us to "start with why." And it's a compelling principle. Knowing why you are doing something is essential to your inspiration and motivation to act. Until the organization knows the *why* of the work, they won't view the work as very important or meaningful. The purpose we selected at Popeyes was "We inspire servant leaders to achieve superior results." What did we believe? We believed that serving performs.

That was our thesis for the turnaround. That was the purpose that rallied people to perform.

But perhaps the most important *why* to understand is why the people come to work. At Popeyes, the Journey to Personal Purpose helped individuals become conscious of their values, their strengths, and their life experiences so that they could articulate why they came to work at Popeyes. This understanding led to a significantly higher level of engagement and commitment to the enterprise.

3. CHOOSE ROAD MAP STRATEGIES: "WHAT"

Decide what needs to be addressed to return the company to a prospering position in the industry. What are the top three to five things that must happen to change the performance trajectory? They should be daring, game-changing ideas, far from the status quo. The strategies become the *what* that you will ask the organization to do. Every strategy has a goal attached to it that defines what a win will look like. There is clarity about the daring destination. At Popeyes, we initially chose brand repositioning, speed-of-service improvement, restaurant P&L improvement, and better real estate selection as our four strategic pillars. These were the vital few, courageous steps we needed to take to get guests back in the restaurant for a better experience and to provide the franchise owners with a viable business model. Basic, but big, steps forward.

4. DETERMINE PRINCIPLES: "HOW"

Carefully select a half dozen principles that will guide *how* you accomplish the work ahead. These are value statements. They tell the organization how to behave and how to arrive at the right decision. If you have a principle of collaboration, it directs the organization to work with others to accomplish the goal. If you have a principle of learning, it suggests that you encourage taking risks and learning from mistakes. To help the organization understand the principle, provide a detailed explanation of what that principle looks like in daily behaviors. Model the principles. Correct when you see errors.

5. SELECT AND DEVELOP LEADERS: "WHO"

Review talent in every area of the organization, looking for the capability you need to execute the strategies and for the character traits you need to live the purpose and principles. Competence is important. Character is even more important. See talent as a full-blown strategy with detailed plans, tools, and systems. Hire a human resource leader with substantial depth of experience in talent management processes. These are not soft skills. These are concrete processes that plan, execute, and track the growth of your leaders. My observation is that few organizations have a rigorous talent management system that is executed consistently.

6. COMMUNICATE CONSISTENTLY AND FREQUENTLY

Leaders often underestimate the importance of good messaging to every stakeholder—to give clarity to the plan and expectations, to inspire and encourage, and to reassure and calm. Develop messaging skills in the leadership of the company through training and real-life practice. Be consistent in messaging so that people remember and trust the direction.

7. TRACK RESULTS MONTHLY, QUARTERLY, ANNUALLY

When I teach on Dare-to-Serve leadership, the audience often thinks the strategy is a "philosophy," not a path to performance. The only way to change that mind-set is to demonstrate results. Start with crisply stated, concrete goals. Create a dashboard to track progress against the goals. When the team falls short of goals, stop and regroup. Find another way to get to the goal. Until performance results occur, you are not serving the people well.

THE LEGACY OF THE LEADER

In wrapping up the Popeyes story, I share with you what I believe is the most important legacy of this leadership team. We taught, encouraged, and prepared dozens of leaders to exhibit Dare-to-Serve leadership. These leaders are now taking those principles far and wide in new leadership roles. In retrospect, the sale of Popeyes has been a "sending out" of leaders who are ready to serve.

From my perspective, the Popeyes story ended too soon, but perhaps the real ending is yet to be written.

In a famous short story by J. R. R. Tolkien, he writes about a painter named Niggle. For some time, Niggle had been obsessed with one particular canvas—a curious picture of a tree with a vast landscape stretching out behind it. But Niggle became too busy, and at the time of his death he had painted only one leaf of this tree that he imagined in his mind. When he arrived in the afterlife, he saw something he recognized, off in the distance. He ran toward it . . . and found the tree, the one he had always imagined, the one he had always planned to paint. The tree was real.

Similarly, I left Popeyes feeling like we had not painted the entire canvas, but I now see that the canvas is much

larger than we thought. Popeyes leaders are now leading teams in other companies with the principles they
learned at Popeyes. They are the "leaves" of the tree we
had imagined. And as they coach and develop the next
generation of Dare-to-Serve leaders, the full image of the
canvas will be revealed.

I can't wait to see that tree in the afterlife.

DARE-TO-SERVE LEADERSHIP LESSONS

The following section shares leadership lessons from former Popeyes leaders:

> *"At Popeyes, we shared the belief that our organization thrived
> because we valued integrity, teamwork, and people. This approach
> allowed us to meet challenges, solve problems, and achieve great
> results. In future leadership positions, I will clearly understand
> the value of assembling, coaching, and developing top talent and
> building broad and trusting organizational relationships as a
> means to success."*

> Sonny Cohen, former general counsel and chief
> administrative officer at Popeyes Louisiana Kitchen

> *"In the early days of the Popeyes turnaround, when we went
> off-site to talk about culture, I thought to myself, Is Cheryl
> serious? Rome is burning and we're in a conference
> room talking about culture. Out of that meeting came our
> purpose and the six principles which became our compass for
> decisions and actions. I know now that Popeyes' success hinged
> on the culture we built. Today I am a CEO with many urgent
> issues, but the first step we took was to create a purpose and a set
> of core values. As a result, I am confident that Granite City can
> create the same focus and results as we did at Popeyes."*

> Dick Lynch, former chief brand officer at
> Popeyes Louisiana Kitchen, now CEO, Granite
> City Food & Brewery

"On reflection, I became a more balanced leader at Popeyes. I learned to better balance the needs of the stakeholder groups. There are always different views as to what is the most important thing, but it is never just one thing. I've learned to balance thinking and doing, people and profits, and the interests of franchisees and investors."

> John Merkin, former chief operating officer, U.S., at Popeyes Louisiana Kitchen, now chief operating officer, Edible International

"Prior to my time at Popeyes, the idea of placing the interests of others above individual interests was foreign to most of the leaders I had met. In fact, contrary to the ubiquitous value statements proudly displayed in corporate hallways, my personal experience was that the majority of companies expected leaders to act in their own self-interest, and structured compensation plans to reinforce this practice. Popeyes was unique in that we shared this view that serving others would ultimately deliver the best results. We looked for a purpose beyond money, and that drove different behaviors and outcomes."

> Andrew Skehan, former president, North America, at Popeyes Louisiana Kitchen, now president, North America, Krispy Kreme

"As a Human Resources executive, you dream of working alongside a team who believes that investing in people and delivering business performance are not mutually exclusive. At Popeyes, every member of the team embraced Dare-to-Serve leadership and challenged themselves to live up to our principles each and every day . . . even when it required difficult decisions, tough conversations, or simply being vulnerable. In my new coaching practice, I am dedicated to helping leaders bring out the best in their teams by leading from the heart and holding teams accountable."

> Lynne Zappone, former chief people officer at Popeyes Louisiana Kitchen, now principal at the Zappone Group

"The first thing I learned was the importance of working collaboratively cross-functionally on one strategic plan, our road map. I also learned the importance of knowing and understanding what motivates your team. Until you know people, you can't expect to access their best work."

> Cheryl Fletcher, former vice president, franchise development, at Popeyes Louisiana Kitchen, now vice president, franchise development strategy, Tropical Smoothie Cafe

"The lesson I took with me from the Popeyes experience was to be true to my purpose and to lead with love. Some viewed Dare-to-Serve leadership as "fluff," when in fact it was about leading with love and holding self and others accountable to deliver results. These are principles that are important to me and are now a part of my leadership approach at my new company."

> Catherine Jefferson, former vice president of people services at Popeyes Louisiana Kitchen, now chief people officer, the Krystal Company

"At Popeyes, I learned that there are many leadership styles that can lead to achievements but there is only one approach where I can both achieve and make a difference in the lives of others. For me, Dare-to-Serve leadership matches my values. I learned to help my team and franchisees grow and reach their potential, listening to them instead of using positional authority to make decisions. As a result, I am both a stronger leader and a better person today. I even use this approach with my kids!"

> Maher Khalifa, former vice president managing director, Europe, the Middle East, and Africa, Popeyes Louisiana Kitchen

"I joined Popeyes because of the people and the mission. I felt at home in a place where fantastic performance was driven by a clear purpose that was expressed in the day-to-day actions of everyone involved. I am now a partner in a strategic communications firm where we lead with respect, integrity, and balance, and I see our team give us and our clients their very best every day. I believe we are part of a movement in business that pushes back against cold, 'bottom-line-only' thinking, and it is driving superior performance."

> Renee Kopkowski, former vice president, communications, at Popeyes Louisiana Kitchen, now president and partner, strat-igence

"When I arrived at Popeyes, in 2016, I quickly recognized that there was something different about this place. Each of the leaders genuinely focused on the success of the people and the enterprise. They demonstrated a genuine desire to listen and understand, before responding. This made me feel that my contributions were valued. This approach to leadership is the legacy that I take from my Popeyes experience."

> John Lukas, former chief technology officer at Popeyes Louisiana Kitchen, now senior vice president of restaurant strategies at Heartland Commerce

"I learned the importance of loving and serving our Popeyes franchisees. I had worked with franchisees for years but had never thought about it this way. Who knew that listening intently, meeting with them regularly, and truly caring about them and their business would lead to incredible relationships and results?"

> Suzanne Miller, former vice president, enterprise planning, at Popeyes Louisiana Kitchen

"My thinking and views on leadership were completely transformed at Popeyes. I learned that leadership carries a lot of responsibility. It needs to be intentional, thoughtful, and provide meaning. The leader needs to earn trust by investing in the team, getting to know them personally, and understanding their purpose or motivation for work. This change in my leadership led to zero turnover and industry-leading results for five straight years."

Hector Munoz, former chief marketing officer at Popeyes Louisiana Kitchen, now executive vice president and global chief marketing officer, Church's Chicken

"I have worked for Popeyes over thirty years, but in the last ten I learned how to shift from an "own it" leader to an "earn it" leader. Owning the results is important, but people follow leaders they trust—and trust is earned."

Tanathan Nelson, former head of company operations–Charlotte at Popeyes Louisiana Kitchen

"I want to lead in a business where, if something isn't right for the people, we don't do it. This was our aim at Popeyes. I have now joined a private company as an equity partner, where we share a belief in this principle and we live it in our daily decisions."

Chris Phillips, former vice president, finance and analytics, at Popeyes, now chief strategy officer, GPS Hospitality

"Popeyes taught me the impact of deep personal connections and the importance of vulnerability and transparency in the leaders. People will go the extra mile for people they connect with. Sharing with vulnerability and transparency breaks down walls and builds deep trust with people. My experience at Popeyes showed me that this creates a place where people thrive and perform."

> Renee Stevens, former vice president of talent, leadership, and culture and former head of people at Popeyes Louisiana Kitchen

"I used to think trust only mattered in personal relationships. I was wrong. Trust is a strategy for increasing team engagement and delivering superior performance. It is a game changer for the organization."

> Brenda Trickey, former general counsel at Popeyes Louisiana Kitchen, now general counsel, Edible International

"The leadership style that made Popeyes successful can be summed up in the title of the leadership class we created: Lead from the Heart. This experience changed the way I think about leadership. When a leader invests in the development and success of their team, the trajectory of the team, and ultimately the company, is forever changed for the better."

> Pete Ward, former deputy general counsel and chief risk officer at Popeyes Louisiana Kitchen, now general counsel, Tropical Smoothie Cafe

"When we began teaching Journey to Personal Purpose at Popeyes, I thought to myself, That won't change much in my leadership approach. *But it did. My personal purpose is to build personal relationships of integrity in order to see positive lasting impact. This purpose continues to ring true in my new role, motivating and convicting me to develop authentic relationships across the organization."*

> Tim Waddell, former vice president of international development at Popeyes Louisiana Kitchen, now vice president, international development, Inspire Brands (parent company of Arby's and Buffalo Wild Wings)

"My richest lesson at Popeyes was recognizing that I attained my greatest personal fulfillment through providing growth opportunities that led to the successes of others. The ultimate form of trust is showing someone your confidence in them to tackle an uncharted opportunity."

> Ron Whitt, former president of International at Popeyes Louisiana Kitchen

These capable leaders leave me with optimism that we started something very special at Popeyes and that it lives on in the lives and leadership of all who shared in the experience.

PART TWO

HOW TO BECOME A
DARE-TO-SERVE LEADER

Everybody thinks of changing humanity,
and nobody thinks of changing himself.
LEO TOLSTOY

I worked many years in large corporations *without ever thinking about my work as "service to others." Early in my career, when people asked me my career philosophy, I would say, "Think like a man, act like a lady, and work like a dog." I took this line from the cover of a book I had never read, yet I quoted the title for twenty years.*

Did I seek the spotlight? I'm sure I did.

Like many, I experienced success: achieving results, getting rewarded, and being promoted. Because my field was marketing and innovation, I enjoyed coming up with bold, daring ideas to grow the business. I enjoyed getting work done in teams. I had plenty of courage, but I'm not sure I had true humility. I did not know that a leader who stepped out of the spotlight to serve others would drive superior performance results. I certainly had not seen a demonstration.

Along the way, I met leaders in nonprofit organizations who were definitely serving others. They ran soup kitchens and homes for abused women. They were missionaries and social workers. I admired their leadership and the profound impact they had on other people's lives. In retrospect, I was probably embarrassed to compare leadership in for-profit companies to this more noble work.

In contrast, my bosses in for-profit organizations were usually focused on getting more of the spotlight for themselves. In fact, most made the spotlight their number one priority. The work environment these leaders created did not lift up and celebrate others. I was embarrassed to call them my role models.

Puzzled by the apparent courage in some leaders and the humility in others, I reflected on what kind of leader I wanted to be.

Conclusion?

The leader must have both—the courage to take the people to a daring destination and the humility to selflessly serve others on the journey. This dynamic tension between daring and serving creates the conditions for superior performance.

I wish I'd figured this out sooner.

CHOOSE TO SERVE

*Do nothing from selfish ambition or conceit, but in
humility count others more significant than yourselves.*

PHILIPPIANS 2:3

IN MY VERY FIRST JOB OUT OF COLLEGE, I was in a meeting
in the corner office with the guy everyone called "the big
boss." The meeting was to make an important decision
on the business. As we huddled around his conference
table, he pondered the facts and said to us, "We need to
do an end run."

I had no idea what he was talking about, so my eyes
quickly and carefully darted around the room to see how
others would react. Would we jump up and run? Would
we duck for cover? Fortunately, all that happened was
that we picked up our papers and went back to our desks.

I needed some training in football terms. I also needed
lessons in leadership.

From that day forward, I have been trying to figure
out leadership. What is it? What are the traits of a leader,
especially leaders who drive superior performance results?

The first place I looked for clues? I studied my bosses.

BOSS OBSERVATIONS

I've never known a person who didn't light up at the memory of a truly great boss. And for good reason: great bosses . . . can shape and advance your career in ways you never expected—and sometimes they can even change your life.

In stark contrast, a bad boss can just about kill you.

JACK WELCH, *WINNING*

About halfway through my career, I worked for two dramatically different kinds of bosses, back-to-back. It was easy to compare them—I worked for the first boss for one year, followed by one year working for the next boss.

I'll never forget my initial meeting with that first boss. When I came to his office, his words to me were, "I chose you for this role. Your talent is just what we need. I look forward to working with you. This is going to be fun." This was a welcome like no other. He was genuinely enthusiastic to have me on his team. I remember thinking that I'd never had a conversation like that before.

For the next year with that first boss, I led a brand-building team that was charged with creating a pipeline of innovative new products. I was supervising the largest group of people of my career thus far. It was a stretch assignment. At home, I was a wife and mother, juggling the demands of family. Life was complicated, but good.

The first boss was interested in all of that. He participated in our new product ideation sessions, encouraging us to be bold and creative. He invested his time in our development as leaders, offering words of wisdom that would shape us for years to come. He seemed to enjoy knowing about our life outside of work—he even had a nickname for my daughter ("Blue Shoes"). During his tenure, our performance results soared. We were the best-performing business unit in the company, and we loved our jobs.

I remember just as clearly the arrival of my second boss. It happened in the second year. He was introduced at a large, company-wide meeting. He gave a speech and said he was excited to be promoted. He had big ambitions.

This boss invited me out for dinner—a "get to know you" opportunity. Somewhere during that dinner, he said, "I've heard you are good. My job is to trip you up." Then he grinned, as if that were a funny thing to say. I've never forgotten those words.

Those words proved to be the second boss's world-view: Find people's faults and errors. Make sure that the people know the boss is smarter and better than they are in every respect. Because the boss is "going places" in the company.

The second boss also decided to invest in my personal development as a leader. He hired an industrial psychologist named Frank, who gave me a series of tests and wrote an eighteen-page report on my personality and opportunities for improvement. My report concluded that I did not read the *Wall Street Journal* enough and that my suits needed an upgrade. I remember that day pretty clearly, too.

A year later, under the leadership of the second boss, this company had lost momentum and most of its leaders had left, including me. A couple years after that, the business was sold to another company.

What did I learn from the contrast between my first and second bosses?

The first boss served the people extremely well, but he was no milquetoast either. He challenged us to pursue bold ideas. He spoke to us with encouraging words that made his confidence in us clear. He also had big aspirations—for the people and for the enterprise. Under his leadership, we accomplished superior performance results. It was one of the best experiences of my career.

DARE-TO-SERVE REFLECTION #22 *Who was your best boss? Who was your worst boss? Which one led you to your best performance results? Why?*

The second boss was plenty smart. He challenged us to do *his* ideas. He spoke to us with condescending words that made it clear he thought we were less capable than he was. He had big ambitions—for his own career. And the performance results tanked. It was one of the worst experiences of my career, and I quit as soon as possible.

This experience was a turning point in my views on leadership. I decided that I wanted to be like boss number 1—"for the people." With equal zeal, I decided that I must avoid at all costs the behaviors of boss number 2 that had killed the energy of the team and led to the end of a top-performing organization.

STUDY OF LEADERSHIP

I began studying different approaches to leadership.

Robert Greenleaf introduced this concept of the servant leader in the late 1970s: *one who leads by putting the well-being of others first.*

Greenleaf was not a professor or a researcher. He was a middle manager in one of the twentieth century's largest organizations, AT&T. He was a thoughtful, optimistic kind of guy who had observed leaders in real-world situations. I think that is why I liked his views. They seemed based on reality.

In his writing, Greenleaf concluded that, at the extremes, a leader chooses to be either Leader First or Servant First—a leader who focuses on self-ambition or a leader whose ambition is to serve others.

The Leader First motto could be "It's all about me": self-focused leadership. This leader seeks a position of power, enjoys getting and wielding power, and seeks to win for personal gain. These leaders have an integrity filter that is selective, meaning they do what is right, as long as it serves them well.

The Servant First motto could well be "It's all about the people": others-focused leadership. This leader is in a position of power but uses the position to share power— listening to people, collaborating with people, and seeking a win for the people and the enterprise. These leaders have moral integrity as their filter. They do what is right, no matter what the cost to self.

Greenleaf said few leaders are actually at the extremes, either one hundred percent Leader First or one hundred percent Servant First.

After forty years of my own observations, I don't think there are "bad guy" leaders and "good guy" leaders. We all have bad and good traits. The problem is that we fail to deliberately decide between the two poles, between self-serving leadership and serving others well. We wobble back and forth between serving the people well and serving our own interests. In fact, we wobble from day to day and hour to hour. We lack conviction about how we lead others.

We struggle between who we are and who we wish we could be.

DARE-TO-SERVE REFLECTION #23 *How would your daily behaviors be different if you put them through a filter of serving others well?*

SHARKS AND DRAGONS

I'm amused by the recent spate of reality shows about business. They reflect the cultural norms about how leaders accomplish great results.

In 2009, ABC launched *Shark Tank,* in which tough, self-made multimillionaires give budding entrepreneurs a chance to secure funding for their business ideas. It is the American version of a global show called *Dragons' Den.* In each episode, the "sharks" confront the flaws in an entrepreneur's concept and we watch as dreams are slayed by dragons. Sharks and dragons leave a clear picture in our minds about business leadership.

These may be our favorite television shows, but do they represent the leaders you want to work for? If not, then we must consider an alternative approach.

Would you be willing to lead differently, to serve others, if it produced superior results?

If so, you will need to avoid these traps.

Serving Trap No. 1: Power I once produced a musical. That's actually not as impressive as it might sound, because, at the time, I was nine years old, at a family reunion.

Even though I was only a kid, I was the oldest child in the group. I decided to name myself as producer and boss. I would pick the play we'd perform and I would assign parts to each of the cousins.

It was 1965, and my favorite movie that year was *The Sound of Music.*

Naturally, *I* was going to sing the title song, so I assigned myself the lead. To help me get into my role, I snuck into my mother's closet and pulled out, as my costume, her wedding dress. All my cousins got lesser roles.

I'm not sure my performance brought tears to the eyes of the adults who had to sit through the play. This I am sure of: At nine years old, I was a power leader. I wielded my power over others to accomplish my desired result. It was all about me. My cousins remind me of this to this day.

Every leadership position comes with some degree of power. The question is, how will a leader use the power he or she has been given?

Leveraging power over others is the primary leadership model celebrated in our culture. We celebrate leaders chasing power, getting power, and wielding power over others. This is what leaders do—or so we think.

We celebrate the trappings of power. Title. Status. Money. Education. Anything that makes it clear that the leader is better than the rest of the people.

Is power a problem only for CEOs? No. All leaders are at risk of grabbing power for their own purposes.

DARE-TO-SERVE REFLECTION #24 *How do you use the power that comes with your position: for personal gain or for serving the people and the enterprise?*

Have you noticed the behaviors of a newly promoted boss in your organization? Do they suddenly act "in charge"? Do they become stern, hands on hips, with a much louder voice? Do they wear the power on their sleeve?

Power over others, the authority you have been given, will be the driver of your leadership unless you make a conscious decision otherwise. Will you use your power for serving others?

Serving Trap No. 2: Achievement In my sophomore year of high school, my family moved to Cupertino, California, where I attended Monta Vista High School. This was an academically challenging school, and I had to step up my game. At the first parents' night, my dad was embarrassed to see that I had not yet passed any of the quizzes in Algebra II/Trigonometry. He let me know that I was grounded until I caught up in math class.

It was a good decision to ground me. I quickly figured out that I needed to study more to get good grades. My dad also provided an incentive, telling me that he would take me out for a fine steak dinner when I received straight As on my report card.

In the spring of my junior year, I achieved the goal of straight As. I made myself a long, pink maxi dress and my dad took me out for a steak dinner at a famous restaurant in San Francisco.

At the age of seventeen, I discovered "personal achievement," and it felt good. But it was all about me. There are still days when I find myself chasing "straight As" and missing the opportunity to serve.

My learning about achievement came from school. Yours may have come from sports or some other form of competition. Wherever you learned achievement, the idea is deeply rooted in your being. Winning is good. Losing is bad.

DARE-TO-SERVE REFLECTION #25 *What is the most important achievement of your life? Was the win for you or for the people on your team?*

There would be no movie named *Chariots of Fire* if Eric Liddell had not won his 400-meter race in the 1924 Olympics. We would not remember Alexander the Great if he had not conquered the Persian Empire. Bill Gates, cofounder of Microsoft, would not be celebrated if his venture had gone bankrupt.

There are no great leaders without great achievements. Achievement is an essential aspect of leadership.

The critical question is *Is the achievement for you or for the people?*

What is your view of achievement? What are you worrying about—your promotion, your next raise, getting recognition, moving to a bigger office?

Your answer?

Serving Trap No. 3: Ambition Upon graduating from college, I started my first job, at Procter & Gamble in Cincinnati, Ohio. My field was called "brand management." There was an entering class of sixty new hires that fall—young college and business school graduates seeking success. I quickly observed that the first big marker in a brand management career was how fast we could reach field sales training. This three-month assignment was required for our first promotion. The sixty of us began to chase that goal to see who would get there first.

I began to learn about ambition. Ambition gave me focus on the future, a goal to shoot for. Work seemed to be measured in salary raises and promotions. My ambition was to reach these milestones and gain the recognition that went with promotions. I had discovered ambition, and I liked it, yet it was all about me.

Ambition is a cultural norm for leadership. Defined by Merriam-Webster as "an ardent desire for rank, fame, or power," the word comes from the Latin word *ambitio*, literally "the act of soliciting votes" for political office. In these roots, we find the problem with ambition. Ambition is a problem if it is all about you.

What would ambition be if it were for the benefit of the people and the enterprise? Perhaps a better word is *aspiration*—for the people we serve. *Aspiration* is "a strong desire to achieve something high or great."

Is it all about your *ambition,* or could we *aspire* to achieve something great together?

DARE-TO-SERVE REFLECTION #26 *Do you have big ambitions for yourself or big aspirations for the people on your team?*

YOUR CHOICE: SPOTLIGHT OR DARE TO SERVE?

What can we conclude about leaders who love the spotlight on themselves? Self-centered leadership is the enemy of high-performing teams.

- It doesn't develop the talents of the people, and it squashes their desire to take risks.

- It may hold people accountable, but it does so without the encouraging words that drive performance.

- It relies on authority, because there are no genuine relationships for influence.

- It is overly confident, without a sound sense of reality, because the followers have stopped talking to the leader.

Self-centered leadership is actually a *lazy* path. The leader merely wields power over others to achieve results for their own benefit. This is not difficult to do. But this approach stunts the performance of the people and the enterprise. It *cannot* deliver superior results.

Dare-to-Serve leadership is much more difficult, and in that challenge, the leader creates the conditions for superior performance:

- It begins with a conscious and humble decision to serve others well.

- It inspires people to pursue a daring destination, an aspiration greater than self.

- It boosts the capability of the people and increases their willingness to take risks.

- It holds people accountable.

- It is appropriately confident.

- It works.

Dare-to-Serve leadership requires deep-rooted personal conviction; it's a demanding path.

The Dare-to-Serve leader has a unique combination of traits—enough courage to take the team to a daring destination and enough humility to serve the people well on the journey. Together, these traits foster the environment for superior performance.

Will you make this more difficult and demanding choice?

Will you choose to serve?

SEVEN

BE **BOLD** AND **BRAVE**

I learned that courage was not the absence of fear,
but the triumph over it. The brave man is not he who
does not feel afraid, but he who conquers that fear.

NELSON MANDELA

A FRIEND OF MINE went bungee jumping in South Africa—jumping off the Bloukrans Bridge, plunging over a spectacular gorge. Rising 709 feet over the Bloukrans River, the bridge is the world's highest commercial bungee jump location (though it is only the thirty-sixth highest bridge in the world). The local operator of this extreme sport has appropriately named his company Face Adrenalin.

When my friend got home from the trip, she showed me the videotape of her jump. During the several minutes of preparation for the jump, while the guides secured her in the harness, my friend screamed and cried as though she were going to die any minute.

I completely relate to that emotion. I probably would have died of fear on the platform. Being much braver than I, my friend made the jump and found herself swinging upside down over Bloukrans River until the crew pulled her back up to the top. She told me how amazing the experience was, how it felt to fly through the air with the blood rushing into her head.

Since I am averse to physical risk taking, this idea of bungee jumping makes absolutely no sense to me. In fact, it seems outright crazy. So why do people take this kind of risk, and what benefits do they get from the experience?

In 2009, Eric Brymer and Lindsay Oades published research on the mind-set and effects of participation in extreme sports. Their findings may surprise you. In the people they interviewed, who pursue sports like BASE jumping, waterfall kayaking, big wave surfing, and extreme mountaineering, the researchers discovered a positive transformation in the *courage and humility* of the participants. Apparently, pursuing activities that involve a real chance of death transforms us in a positive way, increasing our courage for risk taking while humbling us as we realize we do not control the outcomes.

Dare-to-Serve leadership reflects this same paradox.

It requires immense courage and a deeply humble soul at the same time. The leader must call out a daring aspiration for the people—bold enough to risk failure. The leader must give the people confidence that the destination can be reached, yet humbly accept that they do not control all the outcomes. This tension of the uncertain outcome, combined with the leader's commitment to helping the people reach the destination, yields the exciting performance results. Leading is an extreme sport.

LEADERS ARE BOLD

Great leaders have bold ideas—their aspirations for the people are big. Think about leaders in history. Are there any you remember as great who had *small* aspirations for the people?

Gandhi? Mother Teresa? Martin Luther King Jr.?

Even leaders with bad ideas are remembered for their boldness. Hitler? Stalin? Mao?

My first close-up study of daring aspirations in business leadership took place while I was working for Domino's Pizza founder Tom Monaghan. I worked for Tom from 1995 until he sold the company, in 1998, to Bain Capital. I had never been that close to a successful entrepreneur— it was better than any MBA class I ever took.

I once asked Tom what his original aspiration was when he first started the company. It was a daring destination. He said, "I thought I would have one Domino's in every college town in America, which at that time would have been about two hundred." Tom's only other property at this early stage of life was a Volkswagen Beetle, which he owned with his brother, yet he was dreaming big. His bold idea attracted to Domino's entrepreneurs who wanted to be part of making history happen.

Tom's career was a steady stream of bold actions.

Tom was boldly innovative. He once told me that he wasn't much of a marketer. Yet I had already heard the story of how, at the first store, he was hanging Domino's coupons on apartment doors. He marked each coupon with a code number. When a customer purchased a pizza with a coupon, Tom would tally the redemption rates. Tom had no marketing training, but he essentially invented direct marketing years before it came into vogue. Franchise owners used this method to grow Domino's Pizza sales for years to come.

Tom was bold in charitable giving. He was well known as a devout Catholic, one of the largest donors in the Church. It was not unusual to see Cardinal Maida visiting Tom's office in red robes, or to see Tom take a call from the Vatican to handle a request to buy a jeep for nuns in Central America. Tom was bold in giving help to those in need.

DARE-TO-SERVE REFLECTION #27 *How will your daring aspiration for the organization grow the capability and experience of the team?*

Tom was bold with his values at work. He would admit that, in many ways, he fell short in living his values, but he urged Domino's leaders to always aim high. Some of Tom's values were the conventional ones, such as honesty in every action. Some values took a more subtle form, such as paying the company bills immediately. Tom directed the chief financial officer to pay Domino's bills when they arrived, not using the standard cash payment terms. He didn't think it was right to use the supplier's cash to his advantage. Despite the CFO's pleading, Tom held his ground.

Tom's bold vision to build two hundred Domino's was accomplished in 1978. But by the time he sold the company to Bain Capital, there were more than six thousand stores, 1,500 of them outside of the United States. More than a thousand Domino's franchisees were in business as a result of Tom's big idea. The people were served well.

The daring leader helps the people see a future state that is greater than their own imagination and worthy of pursuit. By pursuing a bold aspiration, the people grow in capability and experience, stretching to accomplish things they never dreamed of.

The leader who serves the people well provides a daring aspiration to the organization.

WHAT DARING DESTINATION COULD YOU PURSUE?

As I look back on my early working life, I think my first daring aspiration for the people and the enterprise occurred while working on the Life Savers candy business. (Yes, believe it or not, there is a job growing the Life Savers candy business.) At the time, Life Savers were used largely by grandmothers to keep children quiet at church. It was not a vibrant, growth business.

While I was working on this relatively low-level problem in the 1980s, the president of the United States was thinking about how to prevent missile attacks from other countries, particularly from the Soviet Union. President Reagan set forth a daring aspiration for the nation—it was called the Strategic Defense Initiative (SDI). The idea was that the United States could develop a sophisticated anti–ballistic missile system that would use lasers to shoot down missiles in midair before they reached land.

I remember thinking SDI was a bold, aspirational idea. When it was time to present my bold new ambition for the future of the Life Savers brand, I flew to Norfolk, Virginia, to make a presentation to the senior executives. How did I keep the attention of my audience? I called my presentation the Life Savers Strategic Defense Initiative.

In the presentation, I outlined the team's boldest ideas for rejuvenating the Life Savers brand. There were three: a new candy called Life Savers Fruit Juicers, with 10 percent real fruit juice; a new candy called Life Savers Holes (imagine the dot missing from the center of a Life Saver); and the first U.S. gummi candy, in the shape of a Life Saver—Life Savers Gummi Savers.

Our Life Savers SDI plan did not execute perfectly, but in the end it had good performance statistics.

Life Savers Fruit Juicers played on a trend of the times—adding 10 percent fruit juice to everything in the grocery store. Moms felt better giving their children candy with real fruit juice, and sales and market share increased nicely. Fruit Juicers eventually ran out of steam, but, for a time, it rejuvenated the brand.

Life Savers Holes was complicated. Despite the imaginary idea that every Life Savers candy produced a "hole" with no place to go, the truth was we had to engineer equipment to make hard candy in this very small "hole" format. Then we had to create a plastic package to hold the "holes." Both the candy and packaging equipment were expensive. There was a very tiny bit of candy in an expensive plastic container. Life Savers Holes was launched with much fanfare and excitement, but it ended up as a short-lived fad that fell way short of the returns we had promised.

Finally, we hit the home run idea. Life Savers Gummi Savers was a tender, chewy gummi candy with the amazing flavors you loved in a Life Saver. The only competitors at the time were tough, stale gummi bears imported from Europe. We produced an award-winning advertisement of these squishy candies doing a conga line dance, showing off their tenderness and flavor. The ad won trophies, but, more importantly, the business delivered $100 million in new candy sales.

The Life Savers SDI presentation was boldly ambitious—some would say crazy. Yet it put forth three fresh, innovative ideas. While they didn't all work well or last forever, these new products gave the team new capabilities, new experiences, and new confidence. For the corporation, they delivered sales and profit growth.

DARE-TO-SERVE REFLECTION #28 *Think about a bold initiative that you have been a part of. How did it prepare you well for future leadership?*

At first blush, you might consider it silly to think that a new candy could be called a courageous act that served the people well. I challenge you to think about the effect of this bold ambition on the people. The greatest legacy of this work was the impact of the performance results on the people:

- Engineers created innovative new ways to manufacture candy, growing skills and confidence.

- Manufacturing plants were expanded to make the new products, adding new jobs for people in the community.

- Leaders were promoted to new responsibilities.

- Leaders learned invaluable lessons from the mistakes and failures.

- A brand, Life Savers, was renewed—and serves its customers well to this day.

HOW BRAVE?

Just how brave should your bold idea be? I'm probably not the right person to ask.

One of the bravest ideas ever presented to me was a new invention for keeping pizzas hot. The prototype looked like a sixth-grade science project—complete with visible wires and duct tape holding it together. You needed a lot of imagination to see this as a real possibility.

The invention was a heated disk that, when inserted in a pizza delivery bag, would keep the pizza oven-hot until it reached your front door. When the delivery driver returned to the store, he or she plugged the disk into the wall and it reheated for the next delivery.

The inventor believed that keeping the pizza at the same temperature that it exited the oven—all the way to your home—would be a compelling competitive advantage.

I agreed with him. And my job responsibility at the time was to lead marketing and innovation at Domino's Pizza. Here was my crazy thought . . .

Domino's had invented the thirty-minute delivered pizza—pizza delivered in thirty minutes or it was free. A complicated lawsuit had resulted in the end of that famous thirty-minute guarantee.

Domino's also had a lagging quality reputation—people described it as "the cardboard-tasting pizza I ate in college." Not a compelling reason to buy.

We had just invested in a product improvement to make the crust taste better, but we didn't have a bold new idea to replace the loss of the famous thirty-minutes-or-free guarantee.

When I saw the sixth-grade science project proto-type, I believed we had discovered the answer. Boldly, I presented the heated delivery bag to the executives of Domino's as our next big innovation—explaining the temperature advantage that we could market against competitors, and the advantage of keeping our new, improved pizzas oven-hot all the way to your door.

My peers were now certain that I had lost my mind.

The supply chain executive was concerned about how this equipment would be manufactured and what its failure rate would be. The operations executive thought it was too complicated to handle in the restaurants. The finance executive could not believe that there would be a return on this investment. The franchisee executive was sure that the franchise owners would balk at the capital required to buy this equipment.

DARE-TO-SERVE REFLECTION #29 *What prevents you from pursuing a daring aspiration for the organization? Do you worry that others may think the plan is crazy? Do you have anxiety that you might fail?*

I presented this bold idea seven times to the executive team and CEO Tom Monaghan.

Seven times they rejected the idea, for a whole lot of good reasons.

In a short private conversation with Tom Monaghan, we landed on the questions we had to answer as a team: How will we feel on the day that Pizza Hut is the first to launch heated delivery bags that maintain superior taste and temperature? And what will our franchise owners say then?

Tom, the daring entrepreneur, answered the question with, "We're going to launch the heated delivery bag—and we're going to be first."

The Domino's HeatWave bag was born that day and was launched nationwide several months after that. The technology was new and imperfect. The launch had bumps and costs that many of my peers had forecast. But the bold decision Tom made to launch the HeatWave bag drove sales and market share for the next five years. To this day, it is a competitive advantage that serves the owners and customers of Domino's Pizza well.

GO BIG OR GO HOME

I have a weird personality. I only want to work on big, huge, hard things. Maybe it is my wiring of being an idea person. Maybe it is my love of turnaround opportunities. Maybe it reflects my total lack of patience for slow-moving endeavors.

This I am certain of: I want to work on something that matters. I want to either go big or go home.

On that point, I don't think I'm the only one. I think the people we lead want to work on something that matters. I think the people would rather try something bold and exciting and fail than to never be challenged.

It is the responsibility of the leader to have a daring aspiration for the people and the enterprise. If we don't, the people will not be well served. But I should probably warn you: bold, brave leaders don't win popularity contests.

In business, the bold leaders are described by many as quirky, strange, and even a bit loony. People will say you lack practical knowledge, that you will probably blow the budget, and many other unattractive things. People always have handy the five reasons your idea will fail in the "real" world. People will accuse you of fiscal irresponsibility. The road to bold thinking is paved with doubters and naysayers.

The cheers don't come until the daring idea transforms the organization, rejuvenates a tired brand, or turns around a poorly performing team. Then everyone will cheer the bold idea that saved the day.

If you are a bold leader, with big aspirations for the people and the enterprise, bring your courage and confidence, or your ideas will never leave the paper they are written on.

DARE-TO-SERVE REFLECTION #30 *What is your daring aspiration for your team that is beyond what they know how to accomplish today?*

At the beginning of this chapter, I suggested that pursuing risky activities that involve a real chance of death transforms people in a positive way. The experience builds our courage while humbling us, as we realize we do not control the outcomes.

If you choose to have a daring aspiration for the people and the enterprise, you will step out in courage—and you will be humbled by lessons learned along the way.

Dare-to-Serve leadership is transformative for the leader *and* the followers. In taking a risk, the leader *and* the people stretch and grow, and when they are successful, they experience new confidence and new commitment to the team. They are winners, but they humbly realize that the win would have been impossible by themselves.

Be a bold and brave leader. Serve the people well.

EIGHT

HAVE **CLARITY** OF **PURPOSE**

ABOUT FIFTEEN YEARS AGO, I developed a bit of an obsession. I started asking this question of everyone I met: Why do you work?

I could see them trying to figure out what answer I was looking for. Because that is what we do when we are asked a question—we try to give the right answer.

So they would try to stay calm and say the expected: "I work to put my kids through college." "I work to pay the bills." "I work to support my mother."

These were appropriate responses, even noble.

But the answers gradually reveal that the person doesn't have an answer to the question.

Awkward silence. I could sense them thinking, *What if there is no purpose for my work? What if work is meaningless?*

So I'd change the subject. "How was your weekend?"

I finally met someone who wasn't stumped by the question *Why do you work?*

That someone is Chris. He is my hairdresser.

Chris welcomes me to his chair. He is immensely interested in my day. He offers a neck massage, asks how my haircut is working, and wonders if there is anything about it I want to change? For forty-five minutes, the stressful world evaporates as Chris and I banter. I'm feeling better already. I tease him that I wish I could stop by every day.

When I asked Chris, "Why do you work?," he responded:

> In my twenties I was a partier. I didn't go to college. I didn't have a career plan. I was enjoying life—playing sports and hanging out with buddies.
>
> My parents kept asking me about my plan, but I wasn't too concerned. Then I met this girl I really liked, and she wanted to know my plan. I decided I better get one.
>
> A friend suggested I go to beauty school and make a living cutting hair.
>
> At beauty school, I found I had talent. With training, my skills improved. I discovered that what I loved about the job was this . . .
>
> A woman would sit in my chair—usually stressed, feeling bad about how she looked. She needed encouragement. To face another day, she needed to be renewed.
>
> I started making her renewal my purpose. I saw how she relaxed after a neck massage. I saw how she appreciated me shampooing her hair. I saw how she started to open up and tell me about her life. I found opportunities to tell her she was interesting to talk to. I worked hard to get her hair styled just right—whether she was going out on an important date or not. When she left my chair, I wanted her to feel differently about herself.
>
> Every day I get the opportunity to lift up women— encouraging them, making them feel beautiful. They

leave my chair with confidence, a spring in their step. That is so much fun to watch.

Chris knows exactly what he is doing at work. He knows why he is a hairdresser. He has a purpose.

This purpose has served his clients well—and it has served Chris well. Chris is a top-producing hairdresser in one of the most popular salons in Atlanta. He is booked solid from morning till night and his tips are huge. He is making good money and living a meaningful life.

DARE-TO-SERVE REFLECTION #31 *Why do you work? Do you have a purpose beyond paying the bills?*

Most hairdressers work every Saturday, some Sundays, and the night before every holiday. Chris doesn't. He only works Monday through Friday, a normal work-week, with a back-to-back schedule of women who will wait days just to see Chris.

He serves. He has purpose. He has superior performance results.

PURSUING CLARITY OF PURPOSE

Before you can help others find their purpose at work, you must find your own. The process is no different for you than the team process described in chapter 3. But heed this warning: it is much harder to find clarity in your own personal purpose than to help others find theirs.

Some say that your purpose is easier to identify when you are old. Others say it is easier when you are young. My observation is that, no matter what your age or experience, finding clarity in your personal purpose is just plain hard. It requires honest self-evaluation. It requires a certain transparency to share with others. And, worst of all, it makes us feel vulnerable in front of people—a feeling we find miserable.

My advice? Push through all these barriers to reach clarity of personal purpose. The benefits far outweigh the risks.

EXAMINE YOUR LIFE

I've come to believe that every life has a theme. Sometimes it takes a long time to discover our theme, but if we pause and look back over time, the pattern presents itself in the stories of our lives.

For me personally, leadership is my life theme. You can hear it in the stories of my life.

DARE-TO-SERVE REFLECTION #32 *Looking back over your life, what themes reoccur? How can you use those experiences to positively impact your team?*

It began with the leaders in my family, grandparents and parents who spoke the lessons of leadership into my life. Leadership skills learned while organizing game night at family reunions. Leadership lessons learned by listening to my dad's stories. Leadership experienced as the oldest of four children.

In the workplace, leadership developed as I moved through positions at Procter & Gamble, the Gillette Company, and RJR Nabisco. Leadership lessons gained from working with an iconic entrepreneur, Tom Monaghan.

Leadership refined by the joys and trials of life as a parent of three children.

Until we stop and reflect on our life line, we miss the themes of life experience, themes that could guide us to a clear purpose for our roles as leaders.

Look back over your life experiences and determine the consistent themes that you see in the time line.

CHOOSE YOUR VALUES

I've yet to meet anyone who says, "I have no values." At the same time, I've rarely met anyone who can tell me what their values are—and how they impact their daily work.

What are your values?

Most people will quickly list a few noble values. But you might have to pause and think, if I asked you this question: Are those the values that you use to organize the decisions and activities in your workday? Or are your values less active in your daily work? Do they sit in the background, as aspirations that you hope, over time, will prove true?

To serve others at work, we need to put more thought into the values that govern our day.

DARE-TO-SERVE REFLECTION #33 *How will your top-priority values contribute to the performance of your team and organization? How do you want to be remembered?*

There are numerous exercises for reaching a better understanding of your values. As mentioned in chapter 3, a simple tool is a deck of cards from the John Maxwell organization—thirty-four values, each defined on a card, which makes it easy for you to sort out the ones that are most important to you.

Your task: Decide which *three* values you want to be evident to the people at work. Three values that you want others to hold you accountable to. Three values that you will be remembered for on the day you leave the organization.

For me, personally, after faith and family, the top three values that influence my leadership are:

- Legacy—I want to make a difference in the lives of the people I lead.

- Integrity—I want my daily actions to match my core values.

- Learning—I never want to stop growing and learning new things.

These are not the only values—nor the "best" values. They are simply the three values that I want to be evident in my leadership.

What will yours be?

KNOW YOUR GIFTS

Finding your purpose for work begins with the inner journey of discovering your innate strengths and talents. My hairdresser, Chris, found he was gifted in cutting hair. You may be gifted in teaching, in innovative thinking, in caring for others' needs, or in providing wise counsel.

A landmark book called *Now, Discover Your Strengths*, by Marcus Buckingham and Donald O. Clifton, establishes this premise: you have strengths—find them and put them to work to best serve your team and your organization.

Your workplace typically doesn't talk to you about your strengths. In fact, the traditional annual performance review is usually an hour-long conversation about your weaknesses, euphemistically described as your "opportunities for improvement." This is discouraging and distracting feedback.

DARE-TO-SERVE REFLECTION #34 *What are your best talents that you can offer to the organization? Are you using those talents in your current role?*

At a presentation some years ago on this topic, I heard this statement: "You can spend your whole life working on improving your weaknesses, and gain only a fifteen percent improvement." I can't remember the speaker's name, but I've never forgotten the words.

The speaker continued, saying, "Spend your life applying your strengths, and your contributions will grow exponentially."

This is a life-changing concept at work. To know why you work, you must discover your unique strengths and then spend the rest of your working days offering those strengths to your employer. That is what you are designed to do. Any other path will be frustrating and difficult.

There are numerous talent assessments that can help you discover your most important strengths— StrengthsFinder and StandOut are two of my favorites. For about $15, you can do these assessments online and, within minutes, have clarity about your top five strengths or your top two StandOut roles. I recommend you do this today.

Know your talents and offer them to your organization.

WRITE YOUR PURPOSE

As you increase your understanding of your life experiences, your values, and your strengths, you have an opportunity to bring these lessons together in a statement of your personal purpose.

Your personal purpose is one or two sentences that capture the essence of who you are and how you will serve others. Here are a few examples:

- "To build a sense of community in my team that makes work meaningful and fun."

- "To serve as a trusted advisor wherever I can add value."

- "To give others a sense of dignity—to help them know that their life matters."

- "To teach others to creatively solve problems that others run from."

When you land on your personal purpose, you will have a good reason for going to work each day, a good reason for the time you invest in leading others. When you know your purpose, you will have a way to evaluate whether you are doing what matters most. Without purpose, you will struggle to see any meaning in what you do. The job will simply be a paycheck.

Here's the most important point. If you have no purpose for serving others at work, they will know. *The people know your motive, whether you know it or not.*

A leader without a personal purpose is leading the people on a pointless, meaningless journey. And that's exactly the environment your leadership creates. A meaningless journey . . .

Is that what you want your leadership legacy to be?

Only you can change that outcome for the people you lead. Only you can decide your personal purpose for serving others well.

DARE-TO-SERVE REFLECTION #35 *When will you set aside time to reach clarity about your personal purpose for serving others?*

The Journey to Personal Purpose exercise is available at www.cherylbachelder.com. The one-page format is shown in chapter 3 (see Journey to Personal Purpose Exercise 4).

TEST YOUR PURPOSE

Many have asked me how to make sure their purpose is "true." Out of those discussions came this list of ways to test the genuineness, the authenticity of your personal purpose:

Authenticity test: Find a person who knows you well and tell them your life line, your values, your talents, and your purpose. Ask them if this rings true to who you are. Is this the authentic you?

Others test: Ask yourself, *If I lead like this, will the people I lead be better off?* Leadership is about how you serve others. If your purpose is only about you, revise it.

Action test: Ask yourself, *Now that I have this statement, what exactly will I do differently to make it evident to those I lead?* If you can't determine at least three specific action steps you will take as a result of your purpose, go back and edit it to be so clear and specific that it will drive you to clear action steps.

Hundred-day test: Implement your personal purpose action steps for one hundred days. Then stop and reflect on your purpose. Is it accurate? Is it authentically you? Are there subtle changes you want to make? Edit and try for another one hundred days.

Of these tests, the most important is the action test. For your personal purpose to have an impact on the lives of others, you have to put it to work in your daily life. Organize your calendar with the filter of your purpose. At the end of your day or week, ask yourself, *Did I live my purpose this week? What examples could I give? Did I miss opportunities because I was busy or distracted with other things?*

THE POINT OF PURPOSE

It's not about you.

RICK WARREN, *THE PURPOSE DRIVEN LIFE*

I understand where you might be today. I have been a leader without a personal purpose. I led teams for decades without a clear purpose for serving others well.

Then, while going through a time of struggle and re-flection, I read a book called *The Purpose Driven Life*. The first paragraph reminded me that when you are asked to be a leader, it is for the sake of others; it is not about you. And this changed my approach to leadership forever.

The point of purpose is to determine how you will serve others. If you don't plan to serve, you don't need a purpose.

If you do choose to serve, a personal purpose will determine the focus of your leadership.

During my tenure as CEO of Popeyes, my personal purpose was "To inspire purpose-driven leaders to exhibit competence and character in all aspects of their lives."

This personal purpose was the filter I used for determining how I spent my time in leadership and work. Here are just a few of the ways my purpose guided my work life.

- Mondays and Tuesdays of every week were dedicated to one-on-one coaching sessions with Popeyes leaders, my direct reports. Tuesday mornings were our team meetings to collaborate and make decisions.

- Every six months I chose one vice president–level leader to mentor with six ninety-minute sessions on any topics they chose.

- I toured restaurants each month with the goal of getting to know the restaurant's general manager and finding out how the company could better serve them.

- When asked to speak at public events, I only spoke on the topic of Dare-to-Serve leadership.

Purpose helped me decide what to say yes to. Purpose helped me decide what to say no to.

I enjoyed my work more than ever because I was doing what I cared most about. I also felt my life had more significance because I was singularly focused on how I wanted to make a difference in the lives of others.

Purpose led me to develop deeper, richer relationships at work. Like you, I spent the majority of my waking hours at work. Being intentional about developing future leaders gave me the opportunity to build meaningful relationships with Popeyes leaders and franchise owners.

For me, the most startling outcome of personal purpose was how it changed my performance as a leader. The performance results of Popeyes are by far the most impressive outcomes I have been associated with in my career. I am humbled to realize how long it took me to learn this lesson.

DARE-TO-SERVE REFLECTION #36 *How could your personal purpose change the trajectory of your life?*

Nothing disturbs our soul like the idea of our life being without purpose . . . without impact . . . without meaning. Isn't that our greatest fear?

That we won't be remembered?

That our lives won't make a difference?

That, on the last day, we'll look around and say, "What was that all about?"

We quietly say to our souls, "Please do not let that be the case."

From 2001 to 2009, I encountered a series of life lessons. Nothing is more memorable than the lessons you learn the hard way. I was diagnosed with stage 1 breast cancer; fired from a job that I loved; had teenager challenges with our youngest child; and lost my most important mentor, my father.

Together, these events led me to seek a deeper understanding of my personal purpose in leadership. I decided to lead differently, to challenge myself daily to be more courageous and more humble. For the sake of others.

Don't wait for bad news to develop your convictions about leadership. Personal purpose transforms the focus, capability, and performance of the people.

Clarity of purpose will transform you, too.

NINE

SWITCH FROM *SELF* TO *SERVE*

When we are no longer able to change a situation . . .
we are challenged to change ourselves.

VICTOR E. FRANKL,
MAN'S SEARCH FOR MEANING

IT IS REMARKABLY DIFFICULT TO CHANGE our behavior, because the habits are so deeply engrained in us. It takes very conscious steps to rewire that embedded behavior. And we are hampered by our addiction to those feelings of approval and applause that the world entices us toward—the spotlight. It doesn't sound so thrilling to lay down self-interest and serve others. In fact, it sounds just plain hard.

The first challenge to changing our behavior is accepting this reality: *I'm not inherently good.* I often do not live out what I say I believe. For example, I say I love my spouse and then I do something unloving toward him. I say I am honest and then I hide an important fact from someone so that I look better. I say I have no bias but find myself jumping to an unfair conclusion about another person. Nope, I'm not inherently good. I'm going to need grace and forgiveness in this life. The reality: I'm going to have to keep working on becoming more like those I admire, who serve others with complete disregard for the implications to themselves.

The second challenge is to actually evaluate our behavior, daily, against a set of standards. A powerful example of this premise? The Twelve Steps of Alcoholics Anonymous. For decades, people have embraced these steps as a path to recovery. We can learn from their success. For example, step number 4 is *Take a searching and fearless moral inventory of yourself.* Look at yourself straight in the mirror and tell yourself the absolute truth. Imagine if every leader did that each day, taking a few minutes to reflect and to hold themselves accountable. Have you served the people well this very day? Were you courageous? Were you humble? Where could you have done better? What will you do differently the next time?

What follows are eight examples to encourage you to switch from *self* to *serve* in your leadership. These are practical, specific situations to help you shift your behavior to become a Dare-to-Serve leader.

1. WHAT DOES IT LOOK LIKE TO LOVE THE PEOPLE YOU LEAD?

The voice of *self*: The Human Resources department has sent me endless e-mails reminding me that it is time to do midyear reviews. Are they out of their minds? Don't they understand that summer is when we prepare the five-year plan for the August board meeting? We can't even take a vacation. It's nuts around here. And the last thing I need is another form to fill out. I'll do those reviews when I get around to it.

The voice of *serve*: It is now time for midyear performance reviews; I just received the information from Human Resources. I know how much I appreciate hearing feedback from my supervisor. He did such a good job last year. The conversation helped me understand his expectations, and as a result I was able to exceed my goals last year and receive a good bonus check. I want to be this type of supervisor to my team.

I will set aside an hour for each of my direct reports, and I will prepare a thoughtful review of where they stand on their projects and how they are growing as a leader. Then we will have that important feedback conversation by mid-July, so that they can reflect my feedback in their work in the second half of the year. If I lead this session well, we can probably beat our department goals for the second year in a row. Now that would be something to celebrate!

Will you make the *switch*?

2. WHAT DOES IT LOOK LIKE TO DEMONSTRATE COURAGE IN YOUR PROJECTS?

The voice of *self*: The real problem around here is that we don't have any training materials for our frontline team members. When is someone going to wake up and smell the flowers? If we don't have training materials, we can't be good at our jobs. It's impossible to be successful here. You do your best, and they just tell you that you are falling short. It's depressing. If they aren't going to invest in training materials, we are doomed to failure. I just can't think about this anymore. I'm going to turn up the sound on my earphones.

The voice of *serve*: While touring the stores last week, I saw the new team members struggling to learn the company policies and procedures. They were trying hard to do the job well, but they were lacking the information they needed. I think we could create some simple, low-cost training aids for the stores that would help them learn easily and quickly. I'm going to prepare some examples and take them to the leaders in Operations and Human Resources. They may tell me that we don't have the money for this. But I can offer to pull together a team to create these materials for the stores and improve our company's performance. I also have an idea on how to fund the work. I'm going to get started this afternoon bringing this idea to life.

Will you make the *switch*?

3. HOW COULD I HELP MY TEAM MEMBER DISCOVER AND PURSUE THEIR PERSONAL PURPOSE?

The voice of *self*: That leader of the new system implementation project is a disaster. He is not carrying his weight on this project, and he didn't even come to today's meeting at 2 p.m. Who does he think he is? We have given him a deadline and the resources for getting this done, and he does not seem engaged and owning the outcome. He is just one of those guys that comes to work and goes through the motions, then leaves at 5 p.m. The rest of us aren't going to make our goals if he doesn't step it up.

The voice of *serve*: I was disappointed in the 2 p.m. meeting today on the new system implementation project. For some reason, the team leader didn't attend the meeting. I'm going to call and see if something urgent came up for him, perhaps an emergency.

It turns out that the leader has a rough situation going on at home right now. I had no idea the level of stress he is under. We talked for an hour and I suggested some ways we could adjust his workload. I offered to reassign the implementation project to Jane, to give him some breathing room.

We also talked about the Journey to Personal Purpose class that will be offered next Thursday. Often, when life and work overwhelm us, it really helps to know our *why*. Otherwise it's hard to even get out of bed in the morning. He agreed that looking at his strengths, values, and life experiences was causing him to think differently about work. I suggested that he attend the class and draft his personal purpose. When completed, he can set up time to discuss with me. I can't change things on the home front, but maybe I can help him become more engaged on the project we need to get done this year. It's also a way to let him know how much we care about him—while getting the work done.

Will you make the *switch*?

4. I HAVE THIS PRINCIPLE OF CONTINUOUS LEARNING. IS IT EVIDENT TO MY TEAM?

The voice of *self*: I am the director of U.S. operations and we have been performing very well lately. Speed of service has improved dramatically. One of the trade journals just published an article calling our company "the most improved" on speed of service. But our international team is opening restaurants all over the world, with terrible speed of service to the guests. Don't they understand that this is central to a top-rated quick-service restaurant? I can't believe they haven't asked me for some help.

The voice of *serve*: Recently, the company has been opening a lot of stores in new countries and they have struggled to deliver fast service to the guest. I'm wondering if I could help them with this challenge. While I'm experienced in U.S. operations, I haven't ever been responsible for international operations. My first step will be to travel with the international leader to visit stores in Asia. On this trip, we will tour stores—both ours and the competition's. I'll suggest that we schedule focus groups with customers, employees, and store owners to find out what is on their minds. This should give us a 360-degree view of the challenges we face in delivering fast service. Once we have that input, we can collaborate to come up with some recommendations to improve service times. It sure would be fun to help them reach their performance goals this year.

Will you make the *switch*?

5. AM I COACHING MY TEAM WELL?

The voice of *self*: My team seems to have hit a wall on improving our store performance. Sales are lagging and costs are edging up. I have repeatedly reminded them of the annual goals and their responsibility to hit them. Certainly, they must understand that if they don't improve, they will get fired. At our team meeting tomorrow, I'm going to let them have it.

The voice of *serve*: Store performance is lagging, relative to goals. The team does not seem to have a sense of urgency about fixing the situation. What is it that I need to do differently to help them hit these goals? I have been overcommitted this month and skipped my one-on-one coaching sessions with them. I'm going to schedule a session with each leader on Monday, where I can revisit our goals and ask them questions to determine the stumbling blocks they are facing. I can also encourage them and help brainstorm solutions. That will take a full day, but at the end of the day I'll have a far better understanding of the problem and how I can help them. Plus, they will feel that we are "in this together."

Will you make the *switch*?

6. WHAT IS THE IMPLICATION OF MY PERSONAL PURPOSE ON MY LIFE?

The voice of *self*: I went to this Journey to Purpose class that was required by my supervisor. It was another one of those touchy-feely classes where you are supposed to bare your soul. Now I have this assignment: to take my strengths, values, and life experiences and create a statement of my personal purpose. What a joke. Guess I'll make up something about serving the people well, so that I can turn in my paper and get an A. It's not like it will matter in my day job.

The voice of *serve*: My company offered this class called Journey to Purpose. The leader gave us an entire morning to look at our strengths, our values, and our life experiences—to contemplate what really mattered to us. She explained that the company wanted us to bring our best self to work, and that our supervisors would be in a better position to grow our capability if they understood more about our *why*.

The exercises helped me see a pattern in myself: I'm from a big family. I'm an extrovert. I love to have people over for dinner gatherings. This is because I am so motivated by a sense of community, a sense of sharing life with others. I've never thought of my work this way, but that is what motivates me at work as well. I'm going to look for ways to build community in my workplace. I think that a stronger community will help us reach our performance objectives.

Will you make the *switch*?

7. HOW CAN I DEMONSTRATE ACCOUNTABILITY TO MY TEAM?

The voice of *self*: The franchise owners came to town last week and they were angry. They brought this list of things that needed to be fixed, and they announced their ultimatums. I am so sick and tired of these people hauling off on my team. It was time for them to understand we've had enough. So I told them exactly how I felt. Pounded on the table. Used a few swear words. And then left the room. Let them stew a bit.

The voice of *serve*: I was surprised when the franchise owners came to town last week with a long list of grievances. I had to quickly decide whether to stop and attend to these concerns or to move forward on the agenda I had planned. My team was watching to see what I would do. We have this principle that says we listen carefully. I decided that I must demonstrate this, to be true to our values. So I took the agenda off the table and said, "We need to hear your concerns. We haven't been together for a few weeks, and it looks like some new issues have developed. I'll grab a flip chart and a marker to capture the issues. Would one of you like to start by explaining the first one?"

Will you make the *switch*?

8. DO I TREAT EVERY PERSON WITH DIGNITY, EVEN IN DIFFICULT CIRCUMSTANCES?

The voice of *self*: I need to fire Susan. She's had long enough to figure out this job and she is just not making the cut. It's time to cut her loose. I'll talk to Human Resources today. Maybe they can come up with a way to say we've eliminated her job. Then we wouldn't have to go through a long, stressful performance conversation.

The voice of *serve*: Susan is not performing well. She does not seem to have the skills or the right attitude for this role. We only hired her six months ago. I need to set up a midyear performance conversation with her to better understand the situation and to recommunicate the expectations for this role. It will be important to map out due dates for each of her projects so there is no confusion. I will ask her if there are any obstacles of resources or support that she needs to get the job done. And I will explain that I need her to demonstrate significant improvement in performance in the next ninety days. At the end of the meeting, I'll ask her to prepare a summary of the conversation so that I can make sure that we are on the same page. In ninety days, if there is no improvement, I will know that I did my part to set her up for success.

Will you make the *switch*?

For more examples and more encouragement on your journey, explore the additional applications and resources on the Serving Performs Web site, www. cherylbachelder.com.

TEN

AVOID THE **SPOTLIGHT**

THERE ARE A LOT OF THINGS IN LIFE that I know to be useful and true, but I still don't do them.

I know that keeping your life organized and orderly makes you more effective. But I don't care enough to act on it. I'm just not that bothered by messy desks and messy closets.

I know that budgets are useful planning tools, but I don't care enough to make a budget. For me, it's enough to know that there is still money in my bank account.

Similarly, you are reading about an approach to leadership that drives superior results, but you may not act on this information. You may not switch from *self* to *serve* in your actions.

It all comes down to what you *believe* enough to act on. A belief is something so important to you that when it is violated, you are bothered to a point of distress. You become anxious, even angry. You want to act promptly to rectify the situation.

What beliefs do you care about so deeply that they shape your leadership actions?

My observation is that Dare-to-Serve leaders consciously decide to act on these three core beliefs: *human dignity*, *personal responsibility*, and *humility*. They become so convinced about these beliefs that when they are violated, the leader becomes distressed and quickly adjusts his or her behavior. But don't underestimate the degree of difficulty. First you must *find* your deep-rooted convictions, then you must actually *live them out* in your daily actions.

- For human dignity, you will need to live out the Golden Rule, daily.

- For personal responsibility, you will need to be accountable for your actions, daily.

- For humility, you will need to choose a humble response and apologize when you don't, daily.

Let's dig a little deeper behind each of these beliefs.

HUMAN DIGNITY

Without dignity, identity is erased.
LAURA HILLENBRAND, *UNBROKEN*

The stories of prisoners of war are both heartbreaking and inspiring. Our hearts break for the horrible things done to prisoners to defeat their dignity. And then we hear the story of a prisoner who was not defeated. Through intense focus, meditation or prayer, exercise, and communicating with other prisoners, the person's identity was intact. Their dignity survived. We are amazed at their story.

In these extraordinary circumstances, we can readily agree that every person deserves dignity.

Unfortunately, in the ordinary circumstances of the workplace, we are more careless with human dignity. We spend little time listening to our people. We are impatient with their imperfections. We expect them to listen to our problems and ideas but express no interest in theirs. At the extreme, we humiliate, we publicly criticize and embarrass, we joke in ways that hurt.

Dare-to-Serve leaders care deeply about protecting the dignity of people who work with them. This belief is evident in their daily actions.

They practice a simple rule, the Golden Rule: Do unto others what you would have them do unto you.

This one rule covers a host of circumstances. If you push your daily situations through a filter of what you would like someone to do for you, wouldn't you want to be listened to? Wouldn't you want the boss to be patient with your imperfections? Wouldn't you want them to take time to give you honest feedback and a clear development plan?

In a more difficult situation, where you are not performing up to expectations, wouldn't you want the Golden Rule to apply? Wouldn't you want to know where you stand?

DARE-TO-SERVE REFLECTION #37 *Have you committed to treating every person you lead with dignity, even in difficult circumstances? Could the Golden Rule become a core measure of your effectiveness?*

Every individual, including those having performance difficulties, deserves dignity. They deserve private conversations about the matter, away from public settings. They deserve thoughtful, specific examples to help them understand. They deserve time to absorb the feedback and time to work on personal improvement. If it becomes clear that they cannot stay in the job, they deserve help in understanding what strengths they have that will serve them well in another role.

Most leaders claim to value human dignity; far too many discard it quickly when under pressure at work.

Leaders who are stuck in the spotlight may even ignore or demean other people as a perverse way of keeping the attention on themselves.

Alternatively, if you apply the Golden Rule and treat others as you would want to be treated, you will take yourself out of the spotlight, and better serve your team.

Dare-to-Serve leaders see each individual as a unique and valuable human being, worthy of dignity. And they treat them accordingly.

PERSONAL RESPONSIBILITY

A feature of man's maturity is responsibility towards other people.
DIETRICH BONHOEFFER

In developing Dare-to-Serve leaders, I have witnessed another stumbling block: the absence of personal responsibility. If people believe they have been a victim in this life or if they have a propensity to blame others for their problems, they will struggle to serve others well. It's as if "others" are not even on their radar.

You have witnessed this dichotomy in real life. Two children grow up in the home of a "deadbeat" parent. One child vows to change the course of his life and becomes an effective business and community leader with a healthy marriage and well-adjusted children. But the second child repeats history, becoming another deadbeat parent.

What is the difference between the two people? It is whether they take personal responsibility for their circumstances; whether they think about others, not just themselves.

This pattern exists among leaders. Some take ownership of their leadership and work to become better for the benefit of others. Some never accept responsibility and remain stuck in the spotlight.

Lack of personal responsibility in a leader is just another form of self-absorption. Victim leaders revel in their difficulties and blame the rest of humankind for their troubles. By definition, this thinking blinds them to the fact that the people they serve also have troubles. Such leaders cannot serve others well until they assume personal responsibility for improving themselves and develop empathy for others.

And so it is with Dare-to-Serve leadership. To serve others well, you must look in the mirror—to see your own shortcomings and make the requisite changes in yourself. It is your personal responsibility to do so. You will have no capacity to serve others unless you can take responsibility for your own self.

My dad told me, during my high school years, "After the age of eighteen, you are responsible for your own therapy charges."

Dare-to-Serve leaders accept personal responsibility to improve themselves. They look in the mirror daily. They come to understand their own imperfections, and this builds their empathy for others.

There is a good tool for keeping yourself honest on this point. It is called the Accountability Ladder (see Figure 5), and it was developed by the consulting firm Senn Delaney. It is a structured method for shifting your mind-set from that of an unaware victim to that of a person accepting full responsibility for the next steps.

The way it works? You start at the bottom of the "ladder" and talk yourself out of blame/victim status. Here is an example of how you use the Accountability Ladder, working your way from the bottom to the top:

My childhood home was completely dysfunctional (unaware).

My parents should have been better parents (blame others).

If they had been, I would be more successful (excuses).

That is why I am not getting promoted at work (wait and hope).

But I noticed this other person from the same background was recently promoted (acknowledge reality).

Perhaps if I worked on improving my relationships with others, I would be promoted (own it).

I'm going to ask a few of my closest colleagues for advice on improving relationships (find solutions).

FIGURE 5: The Accountability Ladder

Instead of worrying about getting promoted, I'm going to focus on having better relationships at work. That will improve my results and eventually result in more responsibility (get on with it).

Using the Accountability Ladder, this person has moved from being a powerless victim of circumstances to being a person who owns and acts on opportunities.

DARE-TO-SERVE REFLECTION #38 *Where do you fall on the Accountability Ladder? What are you doing to assume personal responsibility for improving yourself as a leader?*

A leader without personal responsibility remains stuck in the spotlight and fails to serve others well. Dare-to-Serve leaders, however, can't serve others until they have looked at themselves in the mirror, owned their circumstances, and accepted personal responsibility for pursuing solutions or opportunities.

HUMILITY

Humility is not thinking less of yourself;
it is thinking of yourself less.

RICK WARREN, *THE PURPOSE DRIVEN LIFE*

I was once being interviewed for a leadership job in a restaurant company. The interviewer, a senior executive at the company, asked me about my approach to leadership. I said that I developed teams of highly competent people with their egos in check, because I believe humility in leaders leads to better teamwork and better performance. The executive actually leaped out of his chair and said, "That will never work here." Needless to say, I didn't get the job.

In sharp contrast, I remember one of my bosses explaining to me how profoundly he had been impacted by a chapter in *Mere Christianity*, by C. S. Lewis. The chapter title: "The Great Sin." The topic: Pride.

I went home that night and read the chapter. Here are the words of C. S. Lewis that have stuck with me for years: "There is one vice of which no man in the world is free; which everyone in the world loathes when he sees it in someone else; and of which hardly any people . . . ever imagine that they are guilty themselves. . . . There is no fault which makes a man more unpopular, and no fault which we are more unconscious of in ourselves. The vice I am talking of is Pride . . . and the virtue opposite to it . . . is called Humility."

Isn't that the truth? We see pride in others, but we struggle mightily to see it in ourselves. Yet self-centered pride resides in each and every one of us. Humility doesn't come naturally to anyone.

Our self-centered nature can be seen in a two-year-old child in the checkout line at the grocery store, lying flat on the floor, screaming at the top of her lungs, fists clenched because Mom won't buy her a candy bar. The child did not get what she wanted. A temper tantrum followed.

As adults, we have an inner two-year-old. We know what we want, when we want it, and we are despondent, annoyed, and even angry when we don't get our way. It's not appropriate to lie on the floor and scream anymore, but often we are tempted.

True humility is not a destination we are likely to reach in life, but I believe great leaders aspire to be more humble. Humility is not being a doormat; it is simply thinking less about our own needs—and more about the needs of others. When we do this, we exit the spotlight, allowing us to serve others well.

The Dare-to-Serve leader values humility but admits that it is a struggle to be humble. As Lewis commented, "I wish I had got a bit further with humility myself."

I share his view. I am terrible at humility most days. But I know this to be true: followers appreciate humble leaders—leaders with the ability to admit mistakes, to apologize, and to be vulnerable in difficult circumstances; leaders who think of others more than of themselves.

DARE-TO-SERVE REFLECTION #39 *Think of a humble leader whom you deeply admire. What qualities do you see in this person that you want to be evident in your leadership?*

Avoid getting stuck in the self-centered spotlight. Consciously shift the focus to others and see the difference it makes in how you serve. This is the difficult, aspirational work of a Dare-to-Serve leader. You will never claim victory, but your followers will thank you for creating a workplace where they can perform their best.

Early in my career, I attended a two-day workshop on time management skills. When I called home that night, the phone was answered by my three-year-old daughter, Katy. For some reason, I began excitedly sharing with her the things I had learned that day, which I thought would forever change my life.

Katy listened to my thoughts and then responded by sharing the highlight of her day. "Mommy, today I learned this verse at vacation bible school: 'Now that you *know* these things, you'll be blessed if you *do* them' " (John 13:17).

Katy's words ring daily in my ears.

Knowing these things is one thing. Doing them is far more difficult.

Choose the Dare-to-Serve path and be blessed.

CALL TO ACTION

*Leaders are made by other leaders, and are made better
by other leaders, and go on to make yet more leaders.*
ALBERT MOHLER, *THE CONVICTION TO LEAD*

Some years ago, my morning began with a phone call
from a good friend, a mentor and a counselor. He said to
me, "Cheryl, have you considered your influence?"

In my mind, I was thinking, "No, not yet this morning. I am still on my first cup of coffee."

Then he said, "Take the number of employees who
work for Popeyes and multiply that by the number of
hours in a workweek—and then by the number of weeks
in the year."

Head spinning now. Definitely need more coffee.

"You have more influence than you know. Are you
using that influence for good?"

Think about the math:

If you have five full-time people looking to you for
leadership, in the year ahead, you have 10,000 hours of
influence. You will likely spend more time with those
five people than their parents, spouse, teacher, neighbors,
or kids do.

If you have fifty full-time people looking to you for leadership, in the year ahead you have 100,000 hours of influence.

DARE-TO-SERVE REFLECTION #40 *How will you use the opportunity for influence that you have been given? Will you dare to serve?*

If you have five hundred full-time people looking to you for leadership, in the year ahead you have one million hours of influence.

My friend is so right. Every leader has exponential opportunity for influence.

THE STEWARDSHIP OF LEADERSHIP

Business leaders are increasingly the stewards of civilization.
MAX L. STACKHOUSE, *ON MORAL BUSINESS*

In the book *On Moral Business*, Max L. Stackhouse explains that, traditionally, the world's institutions—such as government, family, education, and religion—have been forces for good. What if that role of being stewards of civilization now falls to business leaders? Will we be up to the task?

Business has a prominent role in the world today, driving economic growth in developing nations and teaching future leaders life and work skills. With this opportunity for influence comes a moral imperative to steward the people and the organization well.

Stewarding the future leaders of the world is a significant responsibility.

Your leadership actions will change lives for the better, leave them unchanged, or, regrettably, leave them worse off.

Which will it be?

You have some important decisions to make.

- Will you humbly serve others over your own self-interest?

- Will you pursue a daring destination for the people?

- Will you help others find meaning and purpose at work?

- Will you teach others the guiding principles of serving others well?

In the world today, this kind of leader is in short supply. This is evidenced by the lackluster performance results of many organizations and institutions.

There are not enough Dare-to-Serve leaders to run global businesses. There are not enough Dare-to-Serve leaders to create and operate small businesses. There are not enough Dare-to-Serve leaders to run other institutions, such as government, education, the arts, and charitable organizations.

If there were, the global economy would be growing at an incredible pace. The world's problems would find solutions. The people would be well served. The performance results would be stunning.

The world needs you to become a Dare-to-Serve leader. And then to teach others the same lessons.

I could not be more excited to leave the future in your hands.

Remember, I am the optimist. I believe you will choose to influence and steward the people and the organization well. I believe you will step out of the spotlight and dare to serve.

I wish you great courage and deep humility.

And I promise you this: if you take action on what you have learned, you'll be blessed.

And so will those who follow you . . . for generations to come.

Dare-to-Serve Reflection Questions

Part One: How to Drive Superior Results

CHAPTER ONE: Whom Will We Serve?

#1 *How do you think about the people you lead? Are they a "pain in the neck" or essential to the future success of the organization?*

#2 *Think about difficult leaders you have worked for. Have you made a conscious decision to lead differently than "them"?*

#3 *Who are the most important people you serve—the owner, the boss, the customer, the employees? Which one is your primary focus?*

#4 *What are the specific qualities you love in the people you lead?*

#5 *How do you gain meaningful feedback from those you serve?*

CHAPTER TWO: What Is the Daring Destination?

#6 *What daring destination have you established for your team and organization? What strategies will ensure the team reaches the destination?*

#7 *What are the few vital things that must be addressed in your organization to drive better performance?*

#8 *Have you committed the resources needed to reach the daring destination?*

#9 *What steps have you taken to create a work environment that brings out the best performance from your team?*

#10 *What are the milestones and measurements of progress in your organization? Are you acting on what you learn from the data?*

CHAPTER THREE: Why Do We Do This Work?

#11 *How well do you know the people who work for you? Do you know the three or four events in their lives that have shaped who they are today?*

#12 *If you knew the top-priority values of the people on your team, how would you lead more effectively?*

#13 *Most leaders can tell you the weaknesses of their team members. But can you cite the strengths and talents of your team? Are you accessing their very best capability?*

#14 *What would happen if you helped your team discover and pursue their personal purpose? How would they contribute differently to the performance of the team?*

CHAPTER FOUR: How Will We Work Together?

#15 *What are the principles of your organization? Are they evident in the daily actions of the team members?*

#16 *How is passion demonstrated in the daily actions of you and your team?*

#17 *Are you and your team listening carefully and learning continuously from the people you serve?*

#18 *What process do you have for collecting and analyzing the facts? What process do you have for planning the future?*

#19 *What is your coaching routine? Do you have a specific and thoughtful development plan for each of your team members?*

#20 *How do you hold your team accountable and discourage victim mind-sets or blaming others? How does your team hold you personally accountable?*

#21 *How do you and your team model humility in your daily actions?*

Part Two: How to Become a Dare-to-Serve Leader

CHAPTER SIX: Choose to Serve

#22 *Who was your best boss? Who was your worst boss? Which one led you to your best performance results? Why?*

#23 *How would your daily behaviors be different if you put them through a filter of serving others well?*

#24 *How do you use the power that comes with your position: for personal gain or for serving the people and the enterprise?*

#25 *What is the most important achievement of your life? Was the win for you or for the people on your team?*

#26 *Do you have big ambitions for yourself or big aspirations for the people on your team?*

CHAPTER SEVEN: Be Bold and Brave

#27 *How will your daring aspiration for the organization grow the capability and experience of the team?*

#28 *Think about a bold initiative that you have been a part of. How did it prepare you well for future leadership?*

#29 *What prevents you from pursuing a daring aspiration for the organization? Do you worry that others may think the plan is crazy? Do you have anxiety that you might fail?*

#30 *What is your daring aspiration for your team that is beyond what they know how to accomplish today?*

CHAPTER EIGHT: Have Clarity of Purpose

#31 *Why do you work? Do you have a purpose beyond paying the bills?*

#32 *Looking back over your life, what themes reoccur? How can you use those experiences to positively impact your team?*

#33 *How will your top-priority values contribute to the performance of your team and organization? How do you want to be remembered?*

#34 *What are your best talents that you can offer to the organization? Are you using those talents in your current role?*

#35 *When will you set aside time to reach clarity about your personal purpose for serving others?*

#36 *How could your personal purpose change the trajectory of your life?*

CHAPTER TEN: Avoid the Spotlight

#37 *Have you committed to treating every person you lead with dignity, even in difficult circumstances? Could the Golden Rule become a core measure of your effectiveness?*

#38 *Where do you fall on the Accountability Ladder? What are you doing to assume personal responsibility for improving yourself as a leader?*

#39 *Think of a humble leader whom you deeply admire. What qualities do you see in this person that you want to be evident in your leadership?*

#40 *How will you use the opportunity for influence that you have been given? Will you dare to serve?*

NOTES

The Dare-to-Serve Leader

3 *There's nothing fundamentally wrong* . . . Robert Townsend, *Up the Organization: How to Stop the Corporation from Stifling People and Strangling Profits* (New York: Knopf, 1970), 91.

6 *paradoxical mix* . . . James C. Collins, *Good to Great; Why Some Companies Make the Leap . . . and Others Don't* (New York: Harper Business, 2001), 39.

7 *Leadership Is an Art* . . . See Max De Pree, *Leadership Is an Art* (New York: Crown Business, 2004); C. William Pollard, *The Soul of the Firm* (Downers Grove, IL: ServiceMaster Foundation, 1996); and Rajendra S. Sisodia, Jagdish N. Sheth, and David B. Wolfe, *Firms of Endearment: How World-Class Companies Profit from Passion and Purpose*, 2nd ed. (Upper Saddle River, NJ: Pearson Education, 2014).

PART ONE: HOW TO DRIVE SUPERIOR RESULTS

Chapter One: Whom Will We Serve?

15 *It begins with the natural feeling* . . . Robert K. Greenleaf, *The Servant as Leader* (Atlanta, GA: Robert K. Greenleaf Center for Servant Leadership, 2008), 15.

15 *your attitude is your altitude* . . . A quote similar to "Your attitude is your altitude" is attributed to Zig Ziglar: "Your attitude, not your aptitude, will determine your altitude." See https://www.ziglar.com/category/quotes/.

17 *Leadership Is an Art* . . . Max De Pree, *Leadership Is an Art* (New York: Crown Business, 2004).

22 *Domino's franchisees sued the company* . . . Louise Kramer, "Franchisee Group Hits Domino's with Antitrust Suit," *Nation's Restaurant News* 29, no. 36 (September 11, 1995): 7.

22 *long history of conflict* . . . Bill Carlino, "KFC, Franchisees Settle Lawsuit, Agree to End Bitter 7-Year Feud," *Nation's Restaurant News* 30, no. 8 (February 19, 1996): 1.

22 *troubled franchisee/franchisor relationships* . . . Richard Gibson, "Have It Whose Way?," *Wall Street Journal*, May 17, 2010, http://online. wsj.com/articles/SB10001424052748704869304575109240807702 512; Jason Daley, "Why These 3 Once Thriving Franchises Have Fallen on Hard Times," *Entrepreneur*, August 4, 2014, http://entrepreneur.com/article/235379.

Chapter Two: What Is the Daring Destination?

35 *The bravest* . . . Bayard Joseph Taylor, "The Song of the Camp," in *An American Anthology, 1787–1900*, edited by Edmund Clarence Stedman (Boston: Houghton Mifflin, 1900).

38 *Would you tell me, please* . . . Lewis Carroll, *Alice's Adventures in Wonderland* (Mahwah, NJ: White Seahorse, 2013), 30.

41 *People think focus means saying* yes . . . Steve Jobs, in George Beahm, ed., *I, Steve: Steve Jobs in His Own Words* (Chicago: Agate B2 Books, 2011), 43.

44 *Unless such commitment is made* . . . Peter F. Drucker, *Drucker Management: Tasks, Responsibilities, Practices* (Delhi: Allied Publishers, 1974), 128.

48 *So much of what we call management* . . . Peter F. Drucker, in Kevin Kruse, "100 Best Quotes on Leadership," Forbes.com, October 16, 2012, https: //www.forbes.com/sites/kevinkruse/2012/10/16/ quotes-on-leadership/#9dc04372feb8.

Chapter Three: Why Do We Do This Work?

61 *Most of us* . . . Studs Terkel, *Working: People Talk about What They Do All Day and How They Feel about What They Do* (New York: New Press, 2011), xi.

61 *one in ten Americans* . . . *2017 Restaurant Industry Pocket Factbook*, National Restaurant Association, https://www.restaurant.org/ Downloads/PDFs/News-Research/Pocket_Factbook_FEB_2017-FINAL.pdf.

63   *State of the American Workplace* . . . Available from www.gallup.com.

67   *[Work] is about a search* . . . Terkel, *Working*, xi.

68   *we used a deck of cards* . . . Leadership Values Cards, available from https://store.johnmaxwell.com.

70   *we used an online assessment tool* . . . StandOut, at https://standout.tmbc.com.

Chapter Four: How Will We Work Together?

81   *Alone we can do so little* . . . Helen Keller, in Joseph P. Lash, *Helen and Teacher: The Story of Helen Keller and Anne Sullivan Macy* (New York: Delta/Seymour Lawrence, 1981), 489.

82   *Why not just come right out* . . . James S. Kunen, "Enron's Vision (and Values) Thing," *New York Times*, January 19, 2002, http://www.nytimes.com/2002/01/19/opinion/enron-s-vision-and-values-thing.html.

84   *Nothing great* . . . Ralph Waldo Emerson, "Circles," in *Essays: First Series* (1847). Emerson is here quoting Samuel Taylor Coleridge, *The Statesman's Manual* (1816).

85   *Don't assume* . . . Robert K. Greenleaf, *Servant Leadership: A Journey into the Nature of Legitimate Power and Greatness*, 25th anniversary ed. (Mahwah, NJ: Paulist Press, 2002), 314.

88   *There are abundant current examples* . . . Greenleaf, *Servant Leadership*, 40.

90   *To put it simply and starkly* . . . Larry Bossidy and Ram Charan with Charles Burck, *Execution: The Discipline of Getting Things Done* (New York: Crown Business, 2002), 141.

92   *The price of greatness* . . . Winston Churchill, "The Gift of a Common Tongue," speech given at Harvard University, September 6, 1943, https://www.winston-churchill.org/resources/speeches/1941-1945-war-leader/the-price-of-greatness-is-responsibility.

93   *Ego can't sleep* . . . Stephen Covey, foreword to Robert K. Greenleaf, *Servant Leadership: A Journey into the Nature of Legitimate Power and Greatness*, 25th anniversary ed. (Mahwah, NJ: Paulist Press, 2002), 7.

Chapter Five: What Is the Legacy of a Leader?

97   *Things might have been different* . . . J.R.R. Tolkien, *Leaf by Niggle* (New York: Harper Collins, 2012), 18.

97 *Restaurant Brands in Deal* . . . Sarah Whitten, "Restaurant Brands in Deal to Acquire Popeyes Louisiana Kitchen for $1.8 billion," CNBC (February 21, 2017), https://www.cnbc.com/2017/02/21/restaurant-brands-in-deal-to-acquire-popeyes-louisiana-kitchen.html.

99 *start with why* . . . Simon Sinek, *Start with Why: How Great Leaders Inspire Everyone to Take Action* (New York: Penguin, 2009).

PART TWO: HOW TO BECOME A DARE-TO-SERVE LEADER

113 *Everybody thinks* . . . Leo Tolstoy, "Three Methods of Reform," in *Pamphlets*, trans. Aylmer Maude (Christchurch: Free Age Press, 1900), 29.

Chapter Six: Choose to Serve

116 *I've never known a person* . . . Jack Welch, with Suzy Welch, *Winning* (New York: Harper Business, 2005), 299.

119 *Greenleaf concluded* . . . Robert K. Greenleaf, *Servant Leadership: A Journey into the Nature of Legitimate Power and Greatness*, 25th anniversary ed. (Mahwah, NJ: Paulist Press, 2002), 21–61.

Chapter Seven: Be Bold and Brave

127 *I learned that courage* . . . Jessica Durando, "15 of Nelson Mandela's Best Quotes," *USA Today*, December 5, 2013, http://www.usatoday.com/story/news/nation-now/2013/12/05/nelson-mandela-quotes/3775255.

128 *Eric Brymer and Lindsay Oades* . . . Eric Brymer and Lindsay G. Oades, "Extreme Sports: A Positive Transformation in Courage and Humility," *Journal of Humanistic Psychology* 49 (2009): 114–126.

Chapter Eight: Have Clarity of Purpose

144 *a deck of cards* . . . Leadership Values Cards, available from https://store.johnmaxwell.com.

144 *Now, Discover Your Strengths* . . . Marcus Buckingham and Donald O. Clifton, *Now, Discover Your Strengths* (New York: The Free Press, 2001).

145 *StrengthsFinder and StandOut* . . . See the Gallup StrengthsFinder assessment, at https://www.gallupstrengthscenter.com; and StandOut, at https://standout.tmbc.com.

148 *It's not about you* . . . Rick Warren, *The Purpose Driven Life* (Grand Rapids, MI: Zondervan, 2002), 17.

Chapter Nine: Switch from Self to Serve

153   *When we are no longer able* . . . Victor E. Frankl, *Man's Search for Meaning* (Boston: Beacon, 2006), 112.

Chapter Ten: Avoid the Spotlight

164   *Without dignity* . . . Laura Hillenbrand, *Unbroken: A World War II Story of Survival, Resilience, and Redemption* (New York: Random House, 2010), 183.

166   *A feature of man's maturity* . . . Eric Metaxas, *Bonhoeffer: Pastor, Martyr, Prophet, Spy* (Nashville, TN: Thomas Nelson, 2010), 141.

169   *The Accountability Ladder* . . . See Larry E. Senn and John R. Childress, *The Secret of a Winning Culture: Building High-Performance Teams* (Leadership Press, 1999), 103.

170   *Humility is not thinking less* . . . Rick Warren, *The Purpose Driven Life* (Grand Rapids, MI: Zondervan, 2002), 148.

170   *There is one vice from which no man in the world is free* . . . C. S. Lewis, *Mere Christianity* (Dorset: C. S. Lewis Co., 1952, 1980), 121.

171   *I wish I had got a bit further* . . . Lewis, *Mere Christianity*, 128.

Call to Action

173   *Leaders are made* . . . Albert Mohler, *The Conviction to Lead: 25 Principles for Leadership That Matters* (Minneapolis, MN: Bethany House, 2012), 14.

174   *Business leaders* . . . Max L. Stackhouse, Dennis P. McCann, and Shirley J. Roels, eds., with Preston Williams, *On Moral Business: Classical and Contemporary Resources for Ethics in Economic Life* (Grand Rapids, MI: William B. Eerdmans, 1995), 12.

ACKNOWLEDGMENTS

THIS BOOK WOULD NOT HAVE MADE it into print without the love, encouragement, competence, and support of many people. I am indebted to all those who said an encouraging word, who offered help, who provided feedback, and who brought their own gifts and talents to this process:

To my husband, Chris, for his incredible patience with me during the year that it took to write and publish this book.

To Dr. Robert Thomas, faculty member at the Georgia Institute of Technology, for encouraging me to write this book and for introducing me to Berrett-Koehler Publishers.

To Steve Piersanti, president and publisher of Berrett-Koehler Publishers, Inc., for seeing a place for this book in the marketplace and for giving me the benefit of his wise counsel.

To Mark Levy, book writing coach and magician, for the dynamic way he taught me how to write.

To Bob Berry, for designing the book cover.

To Daniel Watts, my research assistant, and Donna Wilson, my executive assistant, for keeping the project and me on track.

To the servant leaders who have inspired me—Colleen Barrett, Art Barter, Ken Blanchard, Max De Pree, Pat Falotico, Phyllis Hendry, William Pollard, and Andy Stanley.

To the leaders whom I have learned from over the years—Emil Brolick, Doug Conant, Bill Connell, John Cranor, Laurel Cutler, Joel Davis, Patrick Doyle, Louis V. Gerstner, Jr., Aylwin Lewis, Charmaine McClarie, Tom Monaghan, Bob Murray, Denise Ramos, John Seeley, Sally Smith, and Dolph von Arx.

To author friends, who have shared their wisdom— Tony Baron, Shaunti Feldhahn, Don M. Frick, Tim Irwin, Ken Jennings, Larry Julian, Scott MacLellan, Lisa Earle McLeod, and James W. Sipe.

To the former Popeyes board of directors, who supported my decision to write this book in 2014.

To the former Popeyes leadership team for your remarkable contributions to the Popeyes story—I love you very much and deeply appreciate your support.

To the Popeyes franchise owners for being incredible partners in this turnaround story.

To friends and family, who reviewed draft titles, covers, and manuscripts.

To prayer warriors Mark and Debbie McGoldrick, Mac McQuiston, Dawn Routledge, Dick Schultz, and Bob Tiede.

To Jesus Christ for his never-ending presence, love, and grace.

I humbly and gratefully acknowledge that, without all of you, this story could not have been told.

INDEX

ABOUT THE AUTHOR

WHEN MY HUSBAND AND I went to my daughter's third-grade parent–teacher conference, the teacher looked at us and said rather sternly, "I don't know what Tracy is going to be when she grows up, but she is going to be in charge of it." At that moment, I had my first glimpse of what my mother's life must have been like. She raised four children, and we all ended up in charge of something.

I've come to believe that our lives each have a theme, although sometimes it takes a long time to figure it out. At this point, I think it is safe to say that my life theme is *leadership.*

In the first chapter of my life, the theme was expressed by the *leaders in my family*—my grandparents and parents. I was blessed with family leaders who raised us in a safe, loving home, providing a good education, strong faith, and moral values. My father modeled the business leadership traits of competence and character in his career at National Semiconductor Corporation.

In the second chapter of my life, the theme was *learning* leadership—while serving as president of my campus sorority, Sigma Kappa, gaining my business school degrees at Indiana University, and apprenticing with strong leaders in brand management at Procter & Gamble and Gillette. I became fascinated with watching leaders, reading about leaders, and reflecting on leadership. I became a student of leadership.

The third chapter was about *being* a leader in large companies. I became a vice president at the young age of thirty-two and led marketing and product development teams at Nabisco and Domino's Pizza over the next dozen or so years. My career grand finale was supposed to be as president of KFC restaurants, a division of Yum! Brands. But instead, I learned some tough lessons—battling a round with breast cancer and an unsuccessful term as a restaurant company president. I experienced trials in leadership.

Yet another chapter spans the years of my marriage, from 1981 to the present day. My husband, Chris, and I are *coleaders of our family*, raising three daughters with no manual other than the Bible. We've been imperfect parents, but we have loved the responsibility of leading our daughters to faith and to their own life themes. We now enjoy the leadership role of grandparents to the next generation.

As this book tells the story, the capstone lessons of leadership began when I was asked by the board of directors of Popeyes to lead a turnaround of this brand, famous for its Louisiana culinary heritage. This nine-year chapter has been the best leadership opportunity of my life. With a supportive board chairman, a capable leadership team, a distinctive brand, and more than three hundred franchise owners invested for the long haul, we were able to deliver a remarkable set of results. By doing so, we have established one compelling business case for Dare-to-Serve leadership.

I look forward to spending the rest of my days inspiring purpose-driven leaders who exhibit character and competence in all aspects of their lives. This is the calling of my life, and I'm deeply grateful for the opportunity to serve.

WWW.CHERYLBACHELDER.COM

Berrett–Koehler
BK Publishers

Berrett-Koehler is an independent publisher dedicated to an ambitious mission: *Connecting people and ideas to create a world that works for all.*

We believe that the solutions to the world's problems will come from all of us, working at all levels: in our organizations, in our society, and in our own lives. Our BK Business books help people make their organizations more humane, democratic, diverse, and effective (we don't think there's any contradiction there). Our BK Currents books offer pathways to creating a more just, equitable, and sustainable society. Our BK Life books help people create positive change in their lives and align their personal practices with their aspirations for a better world.

All of our books are designed to bring people seeking positive change together around the ideas that empower them to see and shape the world in a new way.

And we strive to practice what we preach. At the core of our approach is Stewardship, a deep sense of responsibility to administer the company for the benefit of all of our stakeholder groups including authors, customers, employees, investors, service providers, and the communities and environment around us. Everything we do is built around this and our other key values of quality, partnership, inclusion, and sustainability.

This is why we are both a B-Corporation and a California Benefit Corporation—a certification and a for-profit legal status that require us to adhere to the highest standards for corporate, social, and environmental performance.

We are grateful to our readers, authors, and other friends of the company who consider themselves to be part of the BK Community. We hope that you, too, will join us in our mission.

A BK Business Book

We hope you enjoy this BK Business book. BK Business books pioneer new leadership and management practices and socially responsible approaches to business. They are designed to provide you with groundbreaking and practical tools to transform your work and organizations while upholding the triple bottom line of people, planet, and profits. High-five!

To find out more, visit **www.bkconnection.com**.

Berrett–Koehler
Publishers

Connecting people and ideas
to create a world that works for all

Dear Reader,

Thank you for picking up this book and joining our worldwide community of Berrett-Koehler readers. We share ideas that bring positive change into people's lives, organizations, and society.

To welcome you, we'd like to offer you a free e-book. You can pick from among twelve of our bestselling books by entering the promotional code **BKP92E** here: http://www.bkconnection.com/welcome.

When you claim your free e-book, we'll also send you a copy of our e-newsletter, the *BK Communiqué*. Although you're free to unsubscribe, there are many benefits to sticking around. In every issue of our newsletter you'll find

- A free e-book
- Tips from famous authors
- Discounts on spotlight titles
- Hilarious insider publishing news
- A chance to win a prize for answering a riddle

Best of all, our readers tell us, "Your newsletter is the only one I actually read." So claim your gift today, and please stay in touch!

Sincerely,

Charlotte Ashlock
Steward of the BK Website

Questions? Comments? Contact me at bkcommunity@bkpub.com.